CREATIVE PAPER CRAFTS

35 Cool, Customizable Projects for Crafty Kids

LISA GLOVER

ROCKRIDGE
PRESS

DEDICATED TO MY DAD

CRAFT PROJECTS

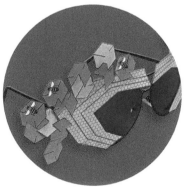

A NOTE TO CRAFTY KIDS

Welcome to *Creative Paper Crafts*!

I'm Lisa the Maker, and I love making things out of paper. Most crafts have to be done at home or in an art studio, but you can make paper crafts almost anywhere.

As a creative kid, I learned that I could jump into the world of paper crafting wherever I went. All it takes to turn paper into anything you can imagine are a few simple tools and a can-do attitude. My folded creations, including my giant cardboard dinosaur costumes, have taken me all over the United States—even to the White House. Yours can take you anywhere you want to go, too.

Maybe you're new to paper crafting, or perhaps you can fold origami cranes in your sleep. Either way, if you're creative and like to try new things, this book is for you.

This book includes 35 cool, unique paper crafts, including a Tiny Ticket Suitcase (page 28), a Solarpunk City (page 23), a Suspicious Rabbit (page 30), and more. Each craft has step-by-step instructions. In the back of the book, you'll find the craft's ready-to-cut template. There are even five bonus templates for more fun!

All you need to complete most of the projects are scissors, a ruler, a pen, and some glue. For the rest, simple household objects, such as paper cups, string, or paper clips, will finish the job.

Every craft is a chance for you to show off your creativity, so keep your colored pencils sharp! There will be patterns to color, islands to arrange, and cats to hide. Read all of the directions for a project before you begin. This will give your ideas every chance they can to shine!

To get started, check out "Tips, Tricks, and Techniques of the Craft" on the next page. This section will set you on the path to success. Be prepared. You're about to make some amazing paper creations!

TIPS, TRICKS, AND TECHNIQUES OF THE CRAFT

This section will prepare you for the adventures ahead. You'll learn how to ready your crafting station and find out what materials you'll need. Then, you'll learn the tips, tricks, and techniques for problem-free paper crafting. Finally, I'll tell you how to copy the templates in the back of this book to keep the fun going.

Your Crafting Station

Work on a table that is flat and at least twice the size of this open book. Find a comfortable chair to sit in. When seated, your elbows should be at about the same height as the table. Make sure you have good lighting so that you can see well.

If you're working at your own desk, keep your materials and tools within reach. For more fun, put crafting materials in cups or recycled containers decorated with colored tape. If your workspace is also the kitchen table, bring out only what you need for each step as you go to make cleanup quick and easy.

To keep your table free from glue and other marks, cover it with a thin cardboard sheet or a craft mat. Find a small box for your paper scraps. You can decorate it to look like a mini recycling bin if you'd like. If you have to stop before finishing a project, keep it safe by putting it on a high shelf or in a container with a lid.

The Materials

To make these projects, you won't need much more than this book. "The Basics" (page v) are the materials that will be used in nearly every project, so make sure you have these before you begin. "The Rest" (page v) includes a short list of objects used in one or two of the projects. You probably already have these at home—in a craft box, the junk drawer, or even the recycling bin. If you don't, they can be found at almost any general store.

THE BASICS

CUTTING TOOLS: The sharpest **scissors** that you feel comfortable using are the best ones. They should fit your hand nicely, so your muscles don't become tired quickly.

ADHESIVE: Small **glue sticks** are great. Liquid glue will work, too. Tacky glue is great for extra hold.

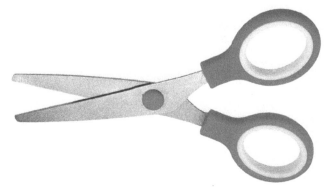

COLORING TOOLS: **Colored pencils**, **markers**, or even **ink pads** are great for expressing your creativity.

PAPER: Even though these crafts come with templates, you may be inspired to create your own. The ones in this book work best on thicker paper called **cardstock**. You can also use copy paper, but your creations will be more fragile. Either of these is good to have if you want to copy designs from this book. Find out more on page viii!

SCORING TOOLS: Folding paper along a line can be tricky. A **ruler** and a **dried-out pen** will help you create score lines to fold along. A bone folder (you can find one at any craft store—just ask!) and a ruler that is see-through make scoring even easier. Learn more about scoring on page vi.

THE REST

- Aluminum foil
- Barrettes
- Cardboard tube
- Clear tape
- Cracker box
- Hair ties
- Hole punch
- Metal snap hair clips
- Mod Podge (or other decoupage glue)
- Paint
- Paintbrush
- Paper clips

- Paper cups
- Paper fasteners (or brads)
- Pen
- Pencils
- Pipe cleaners
- Small ball
- String or yarn
- Sunglasses
- Thin cardboard
- Thin stretchy headband
- Toothpicks

Crafting Types and Techniques

COMMON TECHNIQUES

These techniques will help you build almost every project in the book.

COLORING: If a craft has white space, feel free to color it in. This is best done before building the craft. Test dark colors first on a small area of the template to make sure you can still see the cut and fold lines.

CUTTING: Cut along the solid lines on a template to separate craft pieces from the extra material. For crafts with several pieces, cut all of the pieces out first. If you cut something off accidentally, use tape to reattach it.

SCORING: To make folding easier, score all of the dashed lines first. To do this, line your ruler up with a dashed line and hold it in place with one hand. With your other hand, press down on the end of the dashed line using a dried-out pen or a bone folder, and slide it along the edge of the ruler to create an indent on the dashed line.

FOLDING/CREASING: After scoring the dashed lines, look closely to see if there is an *H* for "hill" or a *V* for "valley" marked on them. These letters tell you which way to fold. To make a hill fold, sometimes called a mountain fold, press the paper on either side of the line down, so that the dashed line is at the top of the "hill." To make a valley fold, press the paper on either side of the line up, so that the dashed line is inside the "valley." Pinch the line and pull your fingers across it, making it sharp. If the instructions tell you to crease the paper, don't worry if it unfolds a little until you know where it goes.

GLUING: Most gray tabs won't be seen in the final craft. Match up these tabs with their corresponding glue spots and line up the edges before gluing in place.

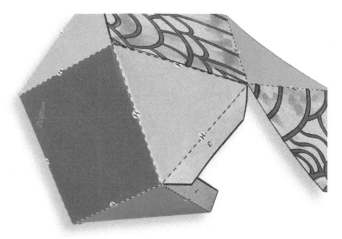

UNIQUE TECHNIQUES AND TYPES

Here are some new and, perhaps, familiar terms and techniques for crafts in the book.

COLLAGE AND SCRAPBOOKING: This art combines words, pictures, and shapes. Before gluing anything down, move the pieces around until you find what looks best to you.

FINISHING: Crafts that you wear or that might get wet will last longer if you protect them with a "finish," or protective coating. Brush on thin layers of Mod Podge or white glue mixed with water, and let dry.

OPTICAL ILLUSIONS: These trick our brains into seeing things that aren't real. A small change can throw off the trick, though. Follow the directions carefully.

ORIGAMI: This is a Japanese art form made by folding a single piece of paper. Traditionally, the paper isn't cut or glued. Fold along the lines carefully. If you make a mistake, take a breath and go back. Smooth the line out as best you can and refold.

POKING HOLES: For larger holes, use a standard hole punch. For smaller holes, carefully twist a fine-point pen point back and forth until it pokes through.

POLYHEDRONS AND SOLID OBJECTS: These 3D shapes are made by connecting the edges of several flat shapes together. Before gluing any edges, loosely form the final shape.

POP-UPS: These change from flat to 3D and back again. Double-check that hidden pieces don't stick out and aren't glued across fold lines. If you make a mistake, carefully pull it apart and try again.

QUILLING: This French and Italian art form is made by rolling and gluing strips of paper into coils. To make different shapes, pinch and push the sides of the coils after gluing.

Reproducing Templates

Use a printer with a scanner to copy templates.

You can also trace the template by hand. Use removable tape to secure the template and a sheet of paper to a window during the daytime. Then use a pencil to draw the lines from the template onto the paper.

Craft Difficulty Levels

On the instruction page for each craft, you'll find a difficulty level: Beginner, Intermediate, or Expert. If you're new to the careful folding needed for paper crafting, you may want to start with "Beginner" crafts such as the Uplifting Envelopes Card (page 1) or the Flipping Zine (page 31). As your paper crafting abilities grow, you can move up to intermediate-and expert-level crafts.

BEGINNER ◼︎   INTERMEDIATE ◼︎   EXPERT ◼︎

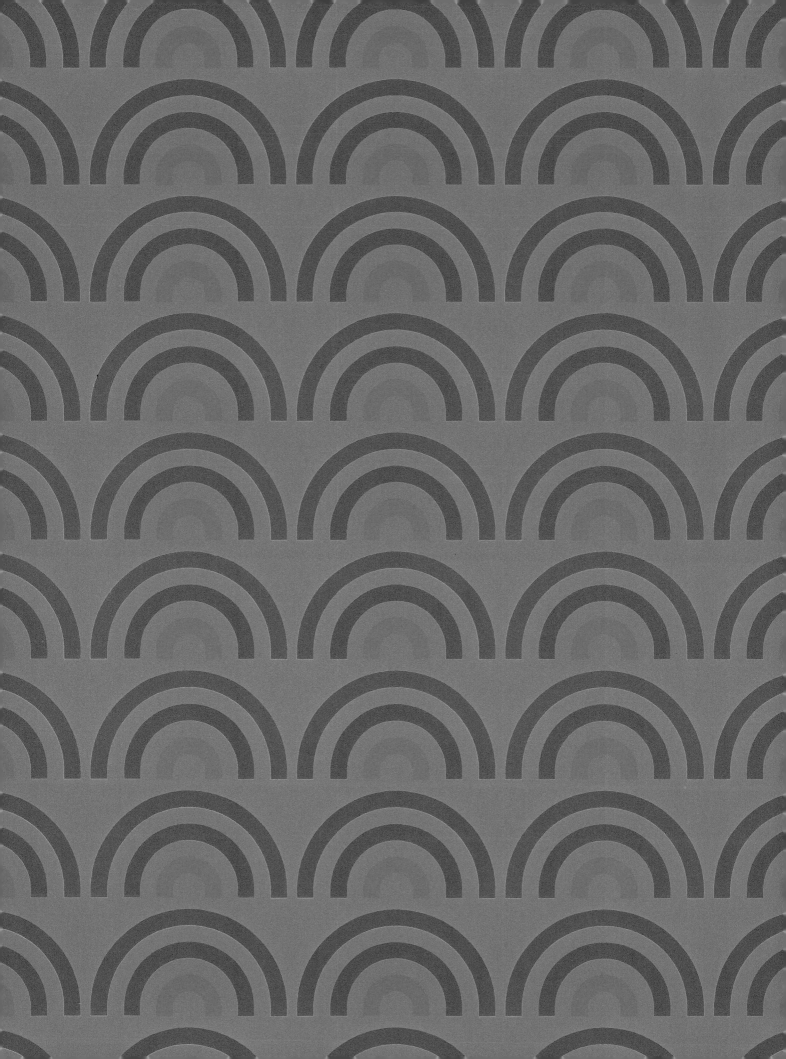

MEMORIES AND KEEPSAKES

UPLIFTING ENVELOPES CARD

TEMPLATE ON PAGE 37

WHAT YOU'LL NEED: scissors, scoring tools, glue, pen

INSTRUCTIONS:

1. Cut out the pieces, following the solid lines.

2. Score and crease along the dashed lines. Fold the **card** piece.

3. Flip an **envelope** piece over and fold in the side tabs (the tabs with gray "Glue" labels). Then, glue the bottom flap to the side tabs and set aside. Repeat with all three **envelopes**.

4. Glue the backs of the **envelopes** to the "strings" on the **card**.

5. Write kind things for someone on the **tiny notes**.

6. Place a **tiny note** in each **envelope**. Fold each top flap closed. Write the name of the person you want to give the card to on the front.

MOUNTAIN PHOTO HOLDER

TEMPLATE ON PAGE 39

COLOR THIS!

WHAT YOU'LL NEED: scissors, scoring tool, glue, thin cardboard

INSTRUCTIONS:

1. Cut out the pieces, following the solid lines.

2. Score and crease along the dashed lines.

3. Match and glue the tab marked **1** on the *outer mountains* to the back of the *left side*. Repeat for tab **2** on the *right side*. Check the picture for placement.

4. Cut out a thin cardboard rectangle the same size as glue spot **3** on the *outer mountains*. Glue it on.

5. Glue tabs **4** and **5** to the inside of the *outer mountains* on each side.

6. Fold up the *inner mountains* and glue tabs **6** and **7** to the inside on each side.

7. Glue the bottom (glue spot **8**) of the *inner mountains* to the middle of the inside of the *outer mountains*.

8. Fold up the front of the *outer mountains* and secure by gluing tabs **9** and **10** on each side.

9. Place your photos in the space created between the outer and inner mountains.

3

5

7

CRAFTING BADGE CASE

TEMPLATE ON PAGE 41

TEMPLATE ON PAGE 41

WHAT YOU'LL NEED: scissors, scoring tool, glue

INSTRUCTIONS:

1. Carefully cut out the badges following the solid lines and being careful not to cut the frame. When you are done with the badges, carefully cut out the remaining white space inside the frame. If you want to make your own badges, trace the template badges on separate paper, cut them out, and color them in.

2. Score and crease along the dashed lines.

3. Glue the tabs on the **background** where marked to the back of the **frame**.

4. Take a **block** and glue the back of the two side tabs to the glue spots on the **background**. The center of the **block** will stick out a bit. Repeat with all of the **blocks**.

5. Glue each **badge** to the glue spot on top of each **block** in any order you like.

COLOR
THIS!

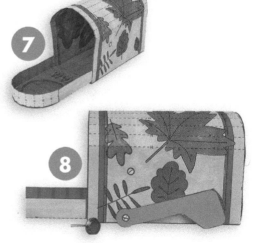

MAPLE LEAF MAILBOX

TEMPLATE ON PAGE 43

WHAT YOU'LL NEED: scissors, scoring tool, glue, pen (for poking hole), paper fastener, cardboard tube, tacky glue

INSTRUCTIONS:

1. Cut out the pieces, following the solid lines.

2. Score and crease along the dashed lines.

3. Glue tab **1** underneath the opposite edge of the **box** piece.

4. Glue all the tabs marked **2** to the remaining open flap.

5. Glue the tabs marked **3** to the back of the **front door** rounded edge.

6. Glue tab **4** into place on the **front door** side panel.

7. Glue tab **5** to the front of the **box**. The **front door** should fit over the **box**.

8. Poke a hole through the X in the **flag** and the **box**, and use a paper fastener to attach the **flag** through the hole.

9. Glue a cardboard tube to the bottom of the **box** using tacky glue.

10. Keep notes you want to remember in the mailbox.

GEOMETRIC GIFT BOX

TEMPLATE ON PAGE 45

WHAT YOU'LL NEED: scissors, scoring tool, glue, string

INSTRUCTIONS:

1. Cut out the pieces, following the solid lines.

2. Score and crease along the dashed lines.

3. Find tab **9** on the *sides* piece, and glue tabs **1** and **2** on the *bottom* piece to the side and bottom of that first white square.

4. Glue tabs **3** and **4** to the next square, **5** and **6** to the next after that, and **7** and **8** to the last.

5. Finally, glue tab **9** underneath the loose purple triangle marked "Sides."

6. To make the *top*, glue each tab labeled "Glue" under the closest purple tab.

7. Place a small gift inside, put the *top* on the box, and tie it closed with string.

COLOR THIS!

POP-UP CARD

TEMPLATE ON PAGE 47

WHAT YOU'LL NEED: scissors, scoring tool, glue

INSTRUCTIONS:

1. Cut out the pieces, following only the outer solid lines.

2. Score along the dashed lines.

3. Fold the **pop-up** in half where you scored it. Cut along the two solid lines on the very top and very bottom of the rainbow.

4. Unfold the **pop-up** and fold it back the other way, creating a valley fold.

5. Open the **pop-up** one more time, and fold the dashed lines on either side of the rainbow.

6. Glue the **pop-up** to the glue area on the **card**.

7. Glue the **add-ons** onto the **card** however you like.

8. Fold up the finished card and give it to someone special.

BONUS TEMPLATE: PAGE 109

FOLDED FIREWORKS FRAME

TEMPLATE ON PAGE 49

TEMPLATE ON PAGE 49

WHAT YOU'LL NEED: scissors, scoring tool, glue, tape, photo, thin cardboard

INSTRUCTIONS:

1. Cut out the pieces, following the solid lines.

2. Score and crease along the dashed lines.

3. Find **firework 1A** and **firework 1B**. Glue tab **1A** to the back of the patterned edge triangle of **firework 1B**. Glue tab **1B** in place behind the patterned edge triangle of **firework 1A**. If you have trouble, check your creases and make sure they are sharp. Repeat with **fireworks 2** and **3**.

4. Tape a photo facedown to the back of the **frame**.

5. Trace the outer edge of the **frame** onto thin cardboard. Cut the cardboard out.

6. Tape the cardboard to the back of the **frame**. Cut out a smaller cardboard rectangle, fold it in half, and tape it on to make a stand for your **frame**.

7. Glue the **landscape**, **fireworks**, and **sparklers** to the front of the **frame**. Trim the **landscape** if needed.

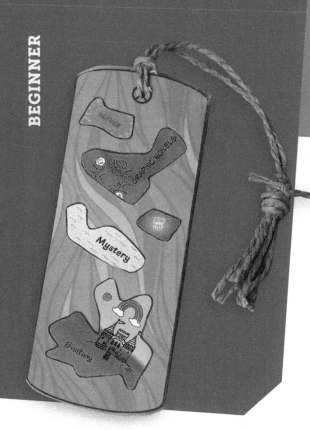

COOL ACCESSORIES

ARCHIPELAGO BOOKMARKS

TEMPLATE ON PAGE 51

• •

WHAT YOU'LL NEED: scissors, glue, clear tape, hole punch, string or yarn

• •

INSTRUCTIONS:

1. Cut out a **bookmark** and several **islands** with the names of book genres you like to read, following the solid lines.

2. Arrange and glue the **islands** to the **bookmark**.

3. Cover the front and back of the **bookmark** in clear tape.

4. Poke a hole through the *X*. Fold a length of string in half, push the folded end through the hole, and pull the two loose ends through the loop. Knot the end.

5. Tie more string to the end of the length. Wrap and knot a piece of string around the top of the tied strings to make a tassel.

6. Repeat steps 1 through 5 to make bookmarks for friends or family members.

2

4

FLIP FOLD BOWS

TEMPLATE ON PAGE 53

••••••••••••••••••••••••••••••••

WHAT YOU'LL NEED:

scissors, scoring tool, glue, metal snap hair clips or barrettes, Mod Podge, paintbrush

••••••••••••••••••••••••••••••••

INSTRUCTIONS:

1. Cut out the pieces, following the solid lines.

2. Score and crease along the dashed lines.

3. Take a **bow** piece and glue one of the sections marked **1** to the patterned section below it. Press tight. Repeat with all of the **1** sections.

4. Flip the **bow** over and finish the pleats by gluing each triangle to the rectangle above it.

5. Glue the back of tab **2** to the top of tab **3**.

6. If you're making a bowtie, clip a metal hair clip over tab **2**. If you're making a hair bow, slide a **barrette attachment** through the upper loop of a barrette and glue the side tabs to the back of tab **2**.

7. To make your bows last longer, finish them by brushing on Mod Podge.

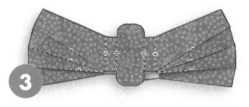

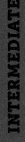
HAUTE HONEYCOMB SHADES

TEMPLATE ON PAGE 55

. . . .

WHAT YOU'LL NEED:

scissors, sunglasses, thin cardboard, glue, scoring tool, tape, Mod Podge, paintbrush

. . . .

INSTRUCTIONS:

1. Cut out the pieces, but for the **bases**, follow only the outer solid lines.

2. Cut the inner sections off the **bases** until they fit the lenses of the sunglasses.

3. Trace each **base** onto thin cardboard. Cut them out. Glue the paper onto the cardboard.

4. Score the dashed lines. Fold each **attachment strip** in half. Glue in place. Fold again in half and glue.

5. Place the **strips** across each **base**. Fold the edges of the **strips** in where they overlap the **bases**.

6. Glue and tape the folded ends to the **bases**. Slide each **base** over an arm of the sunglasses and onto the lens.

7. Match two slots on two **hexagons**. Slide together. Slide more **hexagons** onto the other slots and the **bases**, and glue.

8. Finish with Mod Podge.

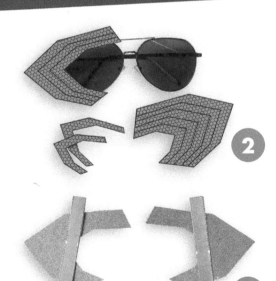

2

5

6

FRIENDLY FOX MASK

TEMPLATE ON PAGE 57

WHAT YOU'LL NEED: scissors, scoring tool, glue, tape, metal snap hair clips, thin stretchy headband

INSTRUCTIONS:

1. Cut out the pieces, following the solid lines. Don't forget the eye holes and between the tabs for the nose.

2. Score and crease along the dashed lines.

3. Glue the front of tab **1** to the back of the **nose**, at the top middle section.

4. Glue the front of tabs **2** and **3** to the back of the **nose**, one on each side.

5. Glue the **right** and **left ears** to the tabs marked on the **face**.

6. Cover both sides of the **attachment strip** with tape. Tape one end of the **strip** to the other end marked "Tape."

7. Tape section **4** to the back of the mask, above the eyes but below the ears.

8. Slide two hair clips onto the **strip**. Clip them to a headband.

9. To wear the mask, put the headband around your head.

COLOR THIS!

QUILL-CHAINS

TEMPLATE ON PAGE 59

WHAT YOU'LL NEED: tape, toothpicks, scissors, glue, paper clips, Mod Podge, paintbrush, hair ties

INSTRUCTIONS:

1. Tape the middle of two toothpicks together to make a quilling tool.

2. Cut out the pieces for one of the quill-chains, following the solid lines.

3. For the circles, glue the *large circle* strips together.

4. To make a coil:

    a. Place the text end of a *quilling strip* faceup in the tool and spin it. Holding the coil tightly, pull it off the tool.

    b. Glue the end of the *strip* to the line where the color changes.

    c. Pinch dashed lines to create a shape. Check against the *guide*.

5. Glue together the matching *bases*, sandwiching a paper clip in between.

6. Glue the coils to the *base*. Finish with Mod Podge.

7. Tie a hair tie to the paper clip to make a keychain.

8. Repeat steps 2 to 8 to make the other quill-chains.

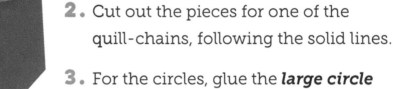

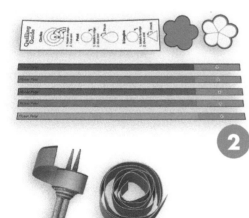

SCALED-DOWN CROWN

TEMPLATE ON PAGE 61

WHAT YOU'LL NEED: scissors, scoring tool, glue, metal snap hair clip

INSTRUCTIONS:

1. Cut out the pieces, following the solid lines. Don't forget the lines on the **crown band** between tabs **1A** and **1B** and between **2A** and **2B**.

2. Score the dashed lines. Fold up all **1** and **2** tabs.

3. Fold the **crown band** lengthwise along the middle dashed line. Glue the halves together.

4. Crease all other dashed lines.

5. Glue each tab **1A** and **1B** to the back of a **short spike**. Then, glue each tab **2A** and **2B** to a **tall spike**.

6. Glue tab **3** to the opposite **band** edge.

7. Fold each **attachment strip** in half. Glue to secure.

8. Match the **4**s and glue together in an *X*.

9. Glue spots **A** through **D** to the spots inside of the **band**.

10. Slide the hair clip around the *X*, and clip it to your hair.

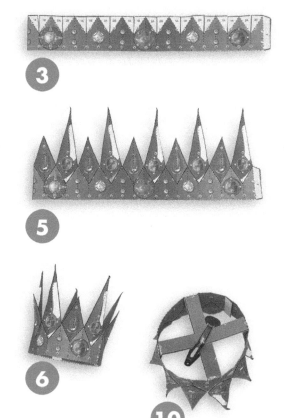

ART AND DECORATIONS

PANCAKE PLANT

TEMPLATE ON PAGE 63

BONUS TEMPLATE: PAGE 111

WHAT YOU'LL NEED: scissors, paper cup, aluminum foil, glue, pipe cleaners

INSTRUCTIONS:

1. Cut off the top half of the paper cup.

2. Crumple up the foil. Place it inside the paper cup.

3. Cut out a few **leaves**, following the solid lines, including the ones in the middle of the circles.

4. Glue each **glue** tab to the back of the cut edge. Press down to secure.

5. To make a branch, cut pipe cleaners to different lengths and twist them together.

6. Poke the pipe cleaner through the yellow center of a **leaf**. Bend it to secure the ends.

7. Poke the branch into the foil so that it stands upright.

8. Repeat steps 3 to 7 until the pancake plant is complete.

HOT-AIR BALLOON

TEMPLATE ON PAGE 65

WHAT YOU'LL NEED: scissors, scoring tool, glue, pen (for poking holes), string, cardstock

INSTRUCTIONS:

1. Cut out the pieces, following the solid lines.

2. Score and crease along the dashed lines.

3. Build **block A** by gluing tab **1** to the opposite cut end. Build **blocks B**, **C**, and **D** the same way.

4. Poke holes through the *X*s on the **balloon** and **basket**. Tie string through the holes to connect them.

5. Glue **blocks A**, **B**, and **C** to the back of the **balloon**. Glue **block D** to the back of the **basket**.

6. Glue the **blocks** to a background made out of a sheet of cardstock.

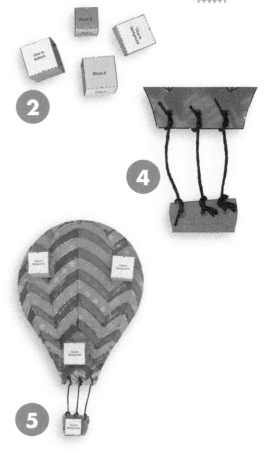

COLOR THIS!

FLEECY ALPACA

TEMPLATE ON PAGE 67

WHAT YOU'LL NEED:

scissors, scoring tool, glue

INSTRUCTIONS:

1. Cut out the pieces, following the solid lines.

2. Score along the dashed lines.

3. Cut along the lines on the **side fleece** and **top fleece** to create a fringe.

4. Rip the **side fleece** into sections. Glue and layer sections of the **side fleece** on both sides of the **alpaca**, being careful not to glue the fringe.

5. Fold up the **alpaca** and glue the heads together.

6. Fold and glue the **top fleece** over the **alpaca**'s back. Fluff up the fringe.

7. Glue on the **add-ons** how you like.

BIRDS-ON-A-WIRE COLLAGE

TEMPLATE ON PAGE 69

WHAT YOU'LL NEED: scissors, glue or Mod Podge, paintbrush

INSTRUCTIONS:

1. Cut out the pieces, following the solid lines. The silhouette of the birds on the wire should be cut out of the background as a single piece.

2. Glue or Mod Podge some *collage pieces* around the silhouette of the birds and the wire.

3. Glue or Mod Podge more *collage pieces* around the first layer, being careful not to glue any over the birds or the wire.

2

ORIGAMI BURST FLOWERS

TEMPLATE ON PAGE 71

WHAT YOU'LL NEED: scissors, scoring tool, pipe cleaners

INSTRUCTIONS:

1. For each *flower*, cut out a square, following the solid lines.

2. Score along the center vertical, horizontal, and two diagonal lines.

3. Crease the four lines you just scored, unfolding each one as you go.

4. Using both hands, push the corners of each square toward each other. Flatten it along the folded lines.

5. Fold **A** to **A** and **B** to **B**. Turn over.

6. Fold **C** to **C** and **D** to **D**. Turn over.

7. Fold **E** to **E** and **F** to **F**. Turn over.

8. Fold **G** to **G** and **H** to **H**. Turn over.

9. Pull on the petals to open the flower. Curl or bend the petals out. Poke a pipe cleaner through the bottom to make a stem.

ACCORDION ARMADILLO

TEMPLATE ON PAGE 73

WHAT YOU'LL NEED: scissors, scoring tool, glue

INSTRUCTIONS:

1. Cut out the pieces, following the solid lines.

2. Score and fold along the dashed centerline on the **body**. Glue the two halves together.

3. Score and crease along the remaining dashed lines.

4. Fold the **head** in half over the marked tab and glue the halves together. Repeat with the **tail**.

5. Match the **foot** pieces to the number on the **body** and glue in place.

GEODE GARLAND

TEMPLATE ON PAGE 75

• •

WHAT YOU'LL NEED: scissors, scoring tool, string, glue, pen (for poking holes)

• •

INSTRUCTIONS:

1. Cut out the pieces, following the solid lines.

2. Score and crease along the dashed lines.

3. Flip a **geode** over. Lay a length of string across it.

4. Glue tab **A** under the closest edge, around the string, forming a little pyramid.

5. Glue tab **B** under tab **C**.

6. Glue the remaining two triangle flaps onto tabs **C** and **D**, around the string. The string should pass through the middle of the **geode**.

7. Poke a hole through the *X* on a **stone**. Thread it onto the string.

8. Repeat steps 3 to 7 on the same string to make a garland.

STARRY NIGHT GLOBE

TEMPLATE ON PAGE 77

WHAT YOU'LL NEED:

scissors, hole punch, paper fastener, tape, glue

INSTRUCTIONS:

1. Cut out the pieces, following the solid lines.

2. Poke a hole through the *X* in piece **1**. Push a paper fastener through this hole from the back.

3. Poke a hole through the *X* in piece **2** and slide it onto the paper fastener. Separate the legs and bend them out about ¼ inch from the head. Tape the legs down.

4. Glue piece **3** to piece **2**. Hold piece **1** steady, and spin the head of the paper fastener. Pieces **2** and **3** should spin.

5. Glue piece **4** to piece **1** along its edge.

6. Glue piece **5** to piece **4**, along the edge. Be careful not to glue it to the inside starry part.

7. Spin the head of the paper fastener. The stars should move in the sky above the town.

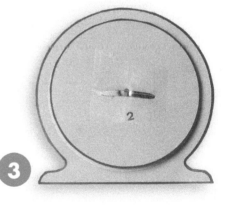

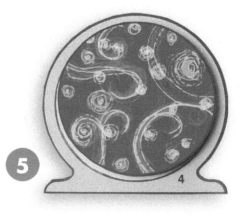

COLOR THIS!

BONUS TEMPLATE: PAGE 113

BOOK NOOK ALLEY

TEMPLATE ON PAGE 79

WHAT YOU'LL NEED: scissors, scoring tool, glue, cracker box, paint, paintbrush

INSTRUCTIONS:

1. Cut out the pieces, following the solid lines.

2. Score and crease along the dashed lines.

3. Pieces **A** and **B**: Glue the **1** tabs to the closest side. Match and glue numbered tabs to the *alley*.

4. Pieces **C** and **D**: Glue each tab **6** behind the closest triangle. Match each piece to its spot on the *alley*, and glue tabs **7** and **8** down.

5. Match and glue tabs **E** and **F** to the *alley*. Glue on *add-ons*.

6. Glue the **9** tabs behind the middle section of the *alley*. Glue the **10** tabs to the third section.

7. Cut out a rectangle 1¼ inches by 4⅜ inches on the cracker box's side. Place the *alley* inside.

8. Glue the remaining tabs to the box around the hole.

9. Paint the box around the hole.

SOLARPUNK CITY

TEMPLATE ON PAGE 81

WHAT YOU'LL NEED: scissors, scoring tool, glue, thin cardboard

INSTRUCTIONS:

1. Cut out the pieces, following the solid lines.

2. Score and crease the dashed lines.

3. *Petra Pavilion*: Glue tab **1** behind the diamond cut edge. Glue tab **2** to the first printed pentagon. Glue tabs **3**, **4**, and **5** under one pentagon each.

4. *Sail Skyscraper*: Glue tab **1** to the opposite edge. Glue the upper center section to the tabs marked **2**. Glue and tuck tab **3** into the top.

5. *Triangle Tower*: Start forming a cylinder. Glue tabs **1**, **2**, and **3** under the opposite diamonds. Glue tab **4** under the opposite triangle. Glue tabs **5** and **6** under the top.

6. Push the *base* tabs on each building through the holes in the *base* piece. Glue underneath.

7. Cut out a thin cardboard circle the size of the *base*. Glue it to the bottom.

PRACTICAL GADGETS

COW CORD KEEPER

TEMPLATE ON PAGE 83

. . . .

WHAT YOU'LL NEED:
scissors, scoring tool,
glue, clear tape

. . . .

INSTRUCTIONS:

1. Cut out the **cow cord keeper**, following the outside solid lines.

2. Score and fold along the dashed hill-fold centerline. Glue the two halves together.

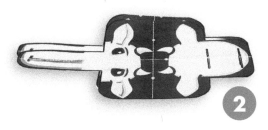

3. Cover the front and back in clear tape.

4. Score and crease the other dashed lines.

5. Fold the **cow cord keeper** in half lengthwise, and cut along the interior solid lines.

6. To use, unfold the **cow cord keeper** and place a folded cord in the middle of the brain. Thread the tongue through both slits in the nose, and gently pull it until the cord is snug inside the head.

COLORED PENCIL TAKEOUT CONTAINER

TEMPLATE ON PAGE 85

WHAT YOU'LL NEED: scissors, scoring tool, glue, hole punch, colored pencils

INSTRUCTIONS:

1. Cut out the pieces, following the solid lines.

2. Score and crease along the dashed lines.

3. Glue the **A** flap to the other **A** flap, **B** to **B**, **C** to **C**, and **D** to **D**.

4. Poke holes through the *X*s in the *noodle tray*.

5. Glue the back of the gray tabs marked **1** on the *noodle tray* inside the *takeout container*.

6. Put colored pencils in the container.

COLOR THIS!

SECRET RUNIC WALLET

TEMPLATE ON PAGE 87

WHAT YOU'LL NEED: scissors, clear tape, scoring tool, glue

INSTRUCTIONS:

1. Cut out the rectangle, following the outside solid lines.

2. Cover both sides with clear tape.

3. Score and fold the **wallet** in half lengthwise. Cut along the solid horizontal line in the middle of the page. Unfold. Cut along the solid vertical line.

4. Score and crease the other dashed lines.

5. Flip the **wallet** over. Fold the top third over to the middle. Fold the middle again over the cut-out V.

6. Fold the inscription up over the top. Glue in place. Tape the right and left sides of the **wallet** closed.

7. Flip over. Fold up the secret code inside the pockets.

8. Fold the **wallet** in half to close it.

9. Use the flaps inside the pockets to write or decode secret notes. Fold it back up to keep it hidden after.

BONUS TEMPLATE: PAGE 115

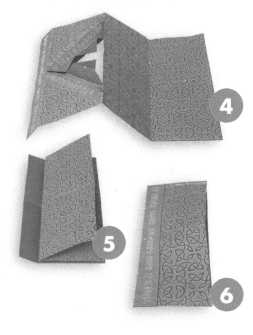

SMARTPHONE MOVIE THEATER

TEMPLATE ON PAGE 89

WHAT YOU'LL NEED: scissors, thin cardboard, glue, scoring tool

INSTRUCTIONS:

1. Cut out the pieces, following the solid lines, except for the gray section on the **screen frame**.

2. Check your smartphone's screen size against the **screen frame**. Cut away the gray shapes one at a time until the opening in the **frame** is about the same size as the screen.

3. Trace the **screen frame** and the **screen holder** onto thin cardboard. Cut them out. Glue the paper pieces onto the thin cardboard.

4. Score and crease the **screen holder** along the dashed lines.

5. Glue the **screen holder** to the back of the **screen frame**.

6. Glue some of the **add-ons** to the **frame**.

7. Start a video on the smartphone. Slide it inside the theater and watch.

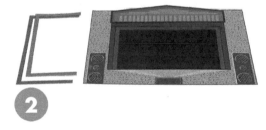

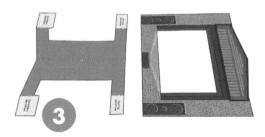

TINY TICKET SUITCASE

TEMPLATE ON PAGE 91

WHAT YOU'LL NEED: scissors, scoring tool, glue

INSTRUCTIONS:

1. Cut out the pieces, following the solid lines.

2. Score and crease along the dashed lines.

3. Fold up *side A* and glue tabs **1**, **2**, **3**, and **4** to their nearest side to secure. Repeat with *side B*.

4. Glue tab **5** on *side B* to inside the bottom flap of *side A*.

5. Glue *add-ons* to the suitcase. Make your own and add them, too.

6. Put your upcoming tickets for movies, concerts, and travel in the case.

FUN AND GAMES

DRAGON FINCH FLYER

TEMPLATE ON PAGE 93

WHAT YOU'LL NEED: scissors, scoring tool, glue, paper clips

INSTRUCTIONS:

1. Cut out the piece, following the solid lines.

2. Score along the dashed lines.

3. Fold along the long diagonal dashed lines on the wings. Fold the **A** tabs.

4. Flip the **dragon finch** over. Fold the triangle at the top.

5. Put glue on the **A** and **B** tabs. Fold the **dragon finch** in half. Pinch tight to glue in place.

6. Fold the wings and the tail flaps. Fold the wing tips.

7. Attach a large paper clip or two small paper clips to the nose.

8. To make the **dragon finch** glide, pinch the belly, pull it back to your shoulder, and throw it straight. Experiment by adjusting the wings, tips, and tail angles to glide in different ways.

SUSPICIOUS RABBIT

TEMPLATE ON PAGE 95

WHAT YOU'LL NEED: scissors, scoring tool, glue

INSTRUCTIONS:

1. Cut out the pieces, following the solid lines.

2. Score and crease the dashed lines.

3. Glue tab **1** on the side of the **body** to the back of the opposite edge.

4. To build the **head**, fold up the face and its side section. Glue tabs **2**, **3**, and **4** behind the side section to secure.

5. Glue tab **5** on the **body** to the back of the chin on the **head**.

6. Place the rabbit on a surface that is a foot or so higher than your head, in an area with even lighting. Close one eye, look in the rabbit's eyes, and move back and forth. The rabbit should look like it is turning its head to stare at you wherever you move. This is called the "hollow face" illusion.

FLIPPING ZINE

TEMPLATE ON PAGE 97

· ·

WHAT YOU'LL NEED: scissors, scoring tool, glue

· ·

INSTRUCTIONS:

1. Cut out the pieces, following the solid lines.

2. Score and crease along the dashed lines.

3. Glue a **page** to the glue tab nearest the page on the **zine spine**, lining the left edge of the **page** up to the fold line. Be careful not to get glue outside of that one tab.

4. Repeat this process with the rest of the **pages**, gluing each to the tab to the left of the previous **page**.

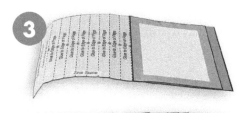

5. Refold along the left edge of each **page** to check that none have become stuck to each other.

6. Glue the **zine cover** to the **zine spine**.

7. Draw a comic on the pages of your zine. Write the name on the cover.

FINGER SOCCER

TEMPLATE ON PAGE 99

WHAT YOU'LL NEED:

scissors, scoring tool, glue, small ball

INSTRUCTIONS:

1. Cut out the pieces, following the solid lines.

2. Score and crease the dashed lines.

3. Glue the top two tabs on the **goal net** under the top flap. Glue the three bottom tabs to the bottom of the **goal base**.

4. On each **shoe**, glue all of the tabs to the inside of the **shoe** sides: front, top, and back.

5. On each **sock**, match up the **A** tabs and glue together.

6. Glue tab **B** to the opposite cut edge, making sure your pointer finger fits inside snugly.

7. Glue a **sock** inside each **shoe**.

8. To play, set up the goal on a flat surface. Put your fingers into the socks and "kick" a ball toward the goal. Give another player one shoe, or build the second set.

BONUS TEMPLATE: PAGE 117

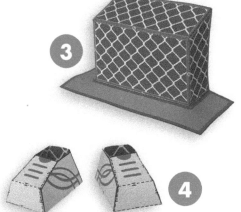

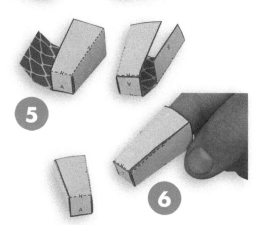

SOLAR SAILER

TEMPLATE ON PAGE 101

WHAT YOU'LL NEED: scissors, scoring tool, glue, Mod Podge, paintbrush

INSTRUCTIONS:

1. Cut out the pieces, following the solid lines.

2. Score and crease the dashed lines.

3. *Hull*: Glue the back of **hull tabs A** and **B** to their matching spots on the **hull**.

4. Glue tabs **C**, **D**, and **E** to the inside sides of the **hull** and tab **F** to the end.

5. Glue tabs **G**, **H**, and **I** to their nearest cut edges.

6. *Sail*: Fold and glue each gray section to the next.

7. *Float bar*: Glue the back of sections **1** and **2**, and **3** and **4**, together.

8. On each end, glue tabs **5** and **6** to their closest edge and **7** to the back.

9. Glue the *float bar* to **J** on the **hull**.

10. Glue the *sail* between sections **2** and **3** and the last tab to the front.

11. Finish with Mod Podge for water resistance.

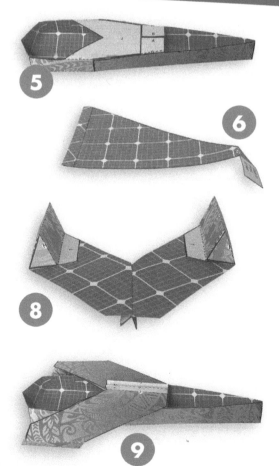

Fun and Games   33

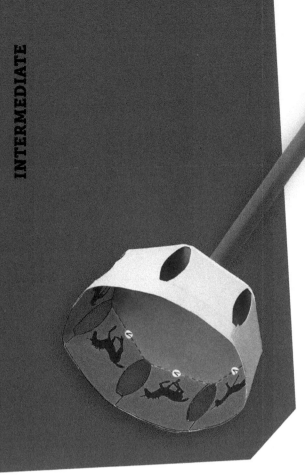

ZOETROPE TOPPER

TEMPLATE ON PAGE 103

WHAT YOU'LL NEED: scissors, scoring tool, tacky glue, pencil

INSTRUCTIONS:

1. Cut out the blue or yellow pieces to make **zoetrope 1** or **2**, following the solid lines.

2. Score and crease along the dashed lines.

3. Glue a **base** to the underside of the **zoetrope**.

4. Flip the **zoetrope** back over. Glue each **glue** tab behind the section next to it.

5. Glue together the two **A** spots on one **strip**. Slide a pencil through the loop.

6. Glue the **strips** together at the **B** spots.

7. Wind the long strip around the pencil to form a tight roll. Glue tab **C** down to the roll and slide it off.

8. Glue the roll to the bottom of the **base** with tacky glue.

9. To use, put the zoetrope on top of a pencil. Spin the pencil between your hands and look through the holes. The images inside should appear to move.

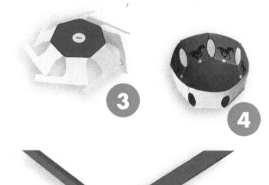

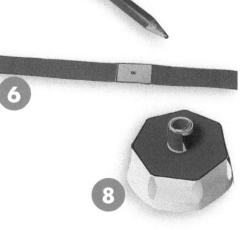

DECISION PRISM

TEMPLATE ON PAGE 105

WHAT YOU'LL NEED: scissors, scoring tool, glue

INSTRUCTIONS:

1. Cut out the pieces, following the solid lines.

2. Score and crease along the dashed lines.

3. Glue tab **A** on the *decision die* under glue spot **G**. Tab **B** goes under "17." **C** goes under "11." **D** and **E** go under "6." **F** goes under "9." Glue spot **G** goes under "5."

4. Glue tab **1** on the *sides* piece under the opposite edge.

5. Glue the *bottom* to the bottom tabs of the *sides*.

6. Place the *decision die* in the prism. Glue the *top* piece to the top tabs of the *sides*.

7. Ask the Decision Prism a yes-or-no question. Shake and roll it like a die. Look at the number that comes up. Whatever is written next to that number in the *key* is your answer.

KEY	
1.	Yes!
2.	Not today
3.	Absolutely
4.	Probably
5.	Don't bet on it
6.	Stormy weather ahead
7.	Definitely
8.	Maybe later
9.	It's a sure thing
10.	Doubtful
11.	Most likely
12.	It is unclear
13.	Try again
14.	There is a way
15.	Without a doubt
16.	It doesn't look good
17.	If you wish it, yes
18.	It is certain

COLOR THIS!

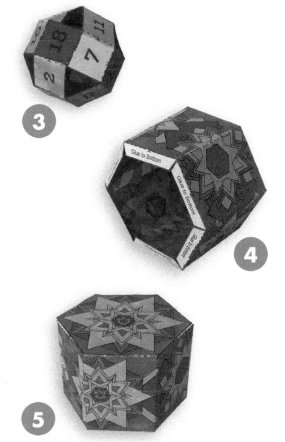

PROJECT
TEMPLATES

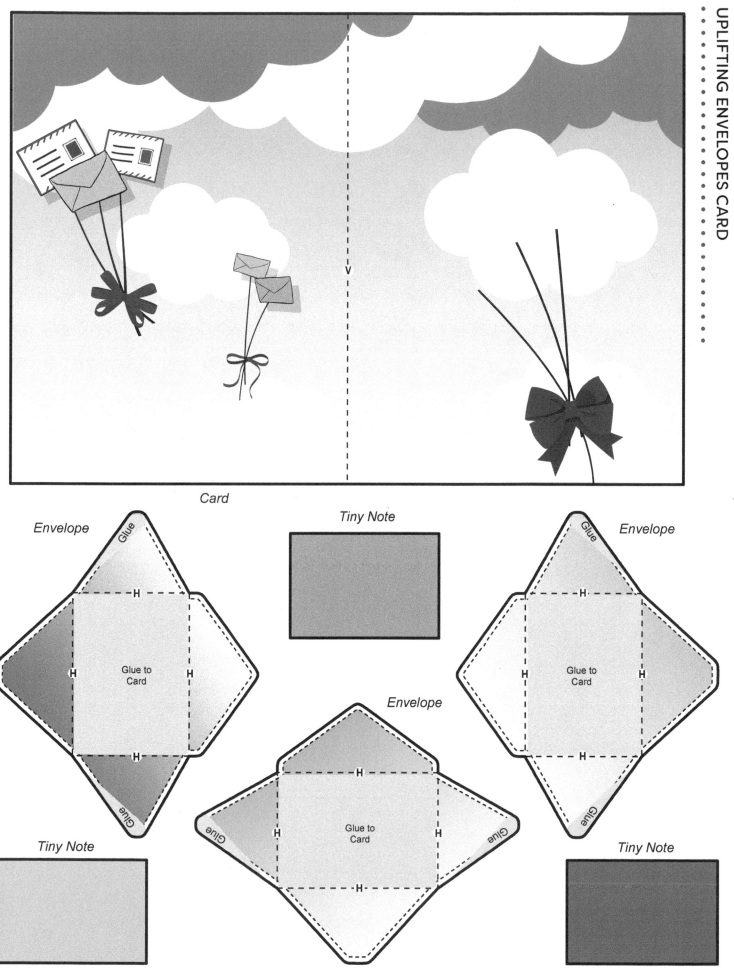

Card

Envelope

Glue

Glue to
Card

H

H

H

H

Glue

Tiny Note

Tiny Note

Envelope

Glue

H

H

Glue to
Card

H

H

Glue

Tiny Note

Envelope

H

Glue

Glue

Glue to
Card

H

H

Glue

Glue

H

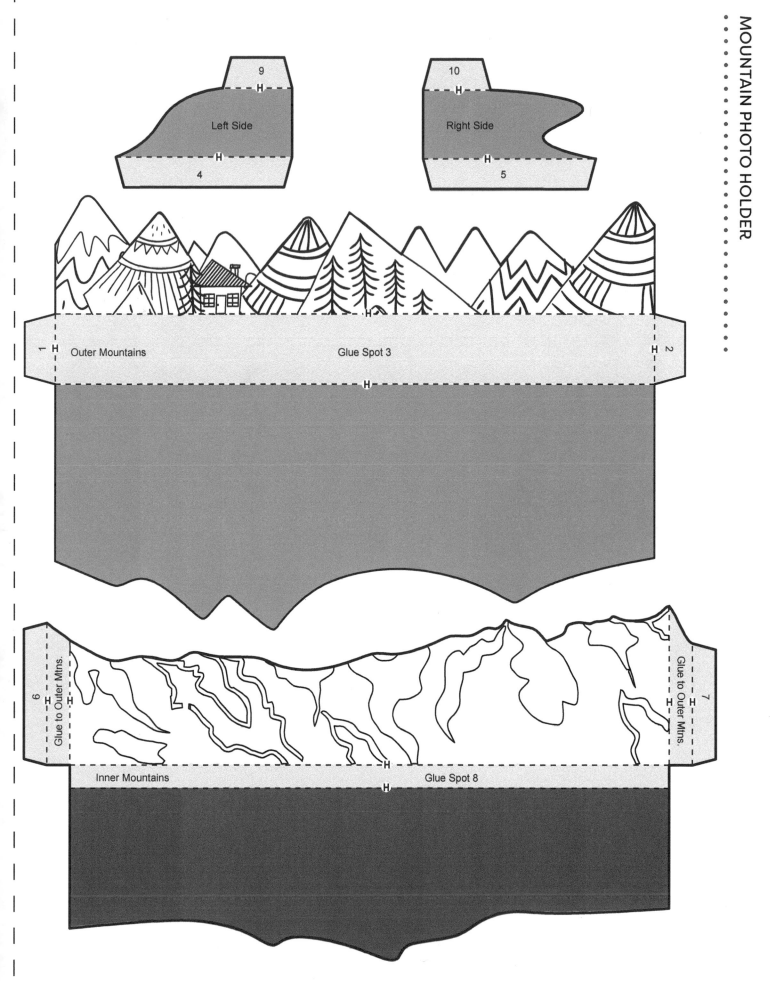

9

Left Side

4

10

Right Side

5

1

Outer Mountains

Glue Spot 3

2

6

Glue to Outer Mtns.

7

Glue to Outer Mtns.

Inner Mountains

Glue Spot 8

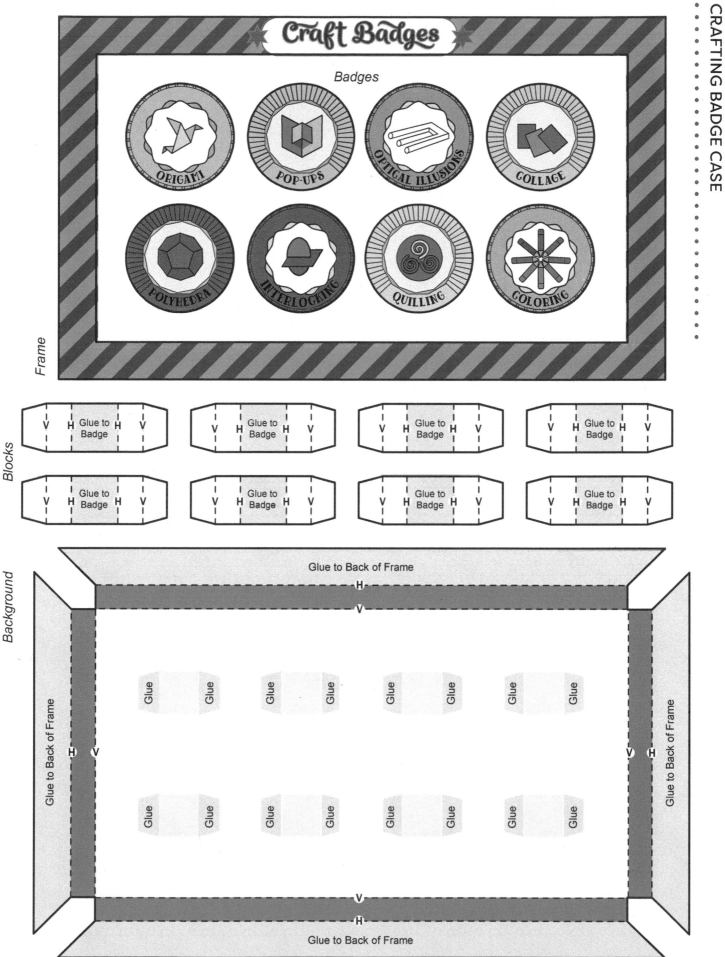

Craft Badges

Badges

ORIGAMI · POP-UPS · OPTICAL ILLUSIONS · COLLAGE

POLYHEDRA · INTERLOCKING · QUILLING · COLORING

Frame

Blocks

Glue to Badge

Background

Glue to Back of Frame

Glue to Back of Frame

Glue to Back of Frame

Glue to Back of Frame

Glue

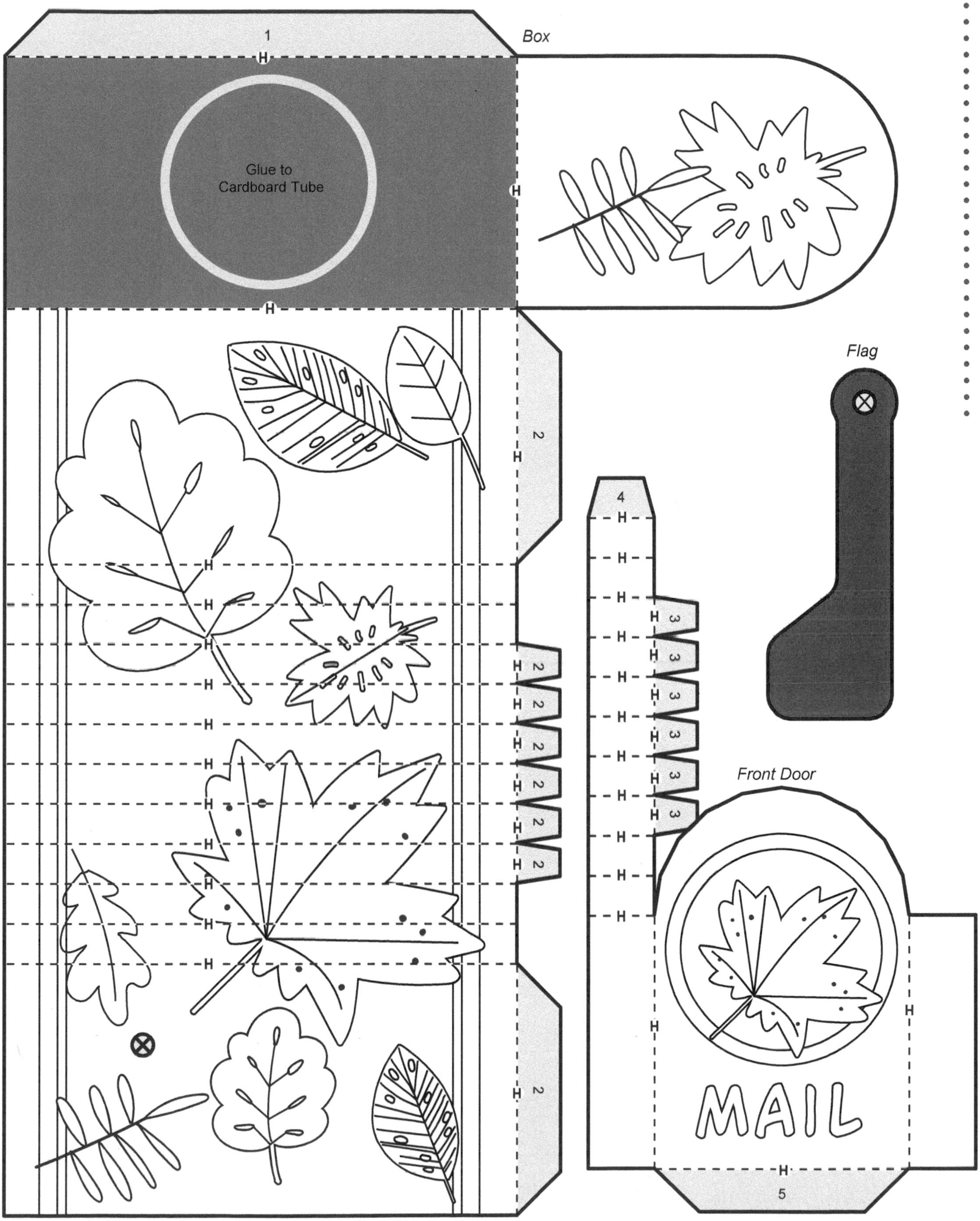

1

Box

Glue to
Cardboard Tube

2

2

4

2
2
2
2
2

3
3
3
3
3
3

Flag

Front Door

MAIL

5

Sides

Bottom

7 H

8 H

9 H

H

H

1

H

H

5 H

2

H

H

4 H

3 H

6

Top

Glue H

H

Glue H

H

H

H

H

H

H

H

H

H

Glue H

H Glue

6 H

Glue to Pop-Up

Glue to Pop-Up

Card

Pop-Up

You bring out my brightest colors

Add-Ons

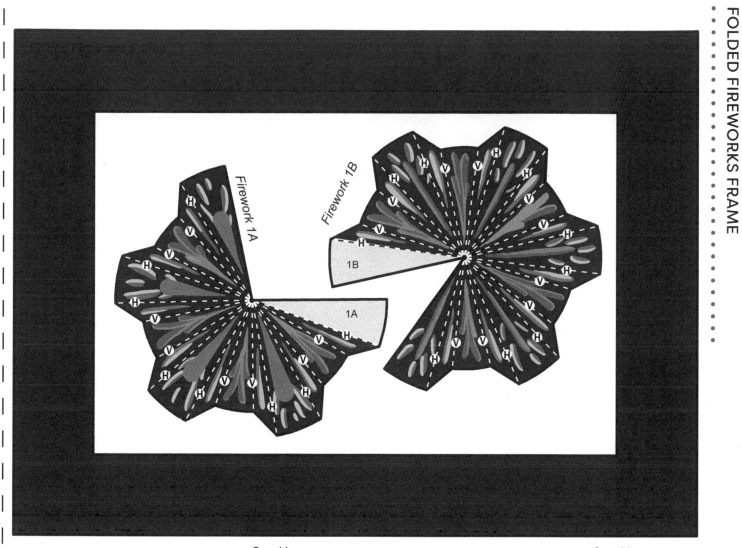

Folded Fireworks Frame

Firework 1A

Firework 1B

1B

1A

Firework 2A

2A

Sparkler

Firework 3A

3A

Sparkler

Firework 2B

2B

Sparkler

Firework 3B

3B

Sparkler

Landscape

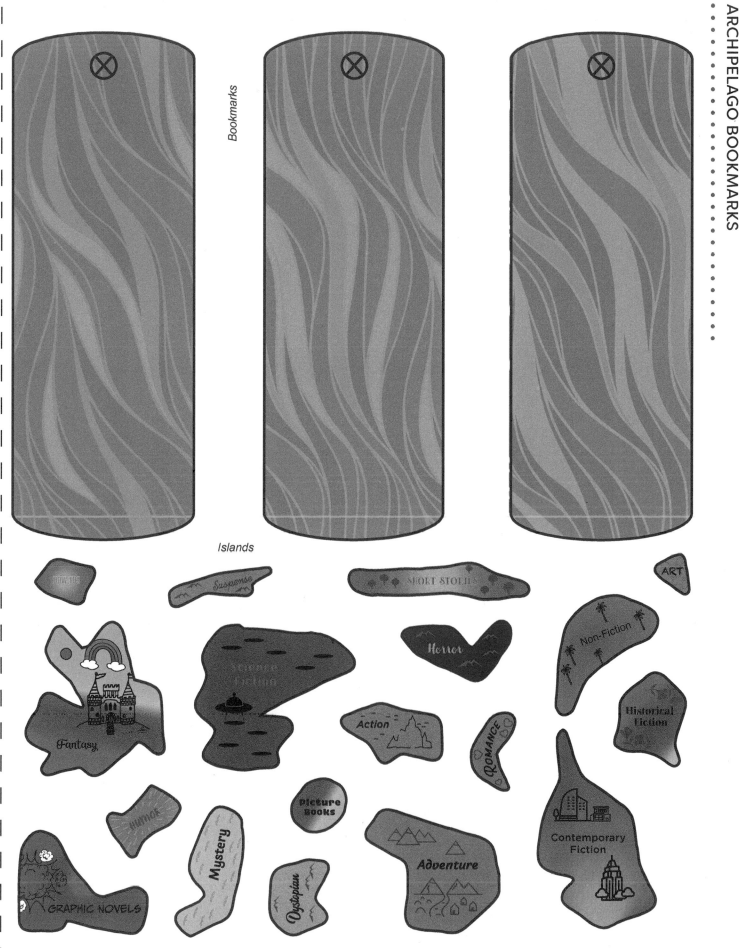

Bookmarks

Islands

HOW-TOs
Suspense
SHORT STORIES
ART
Non-Fiction
Horror
Fantasy
Science Fiction
Action
Romance
Historical Fiction
Humor
Picture Books
Mystery
Dystopian
Adventure
Contemporary Fiction
GRAPHIC NOVELS

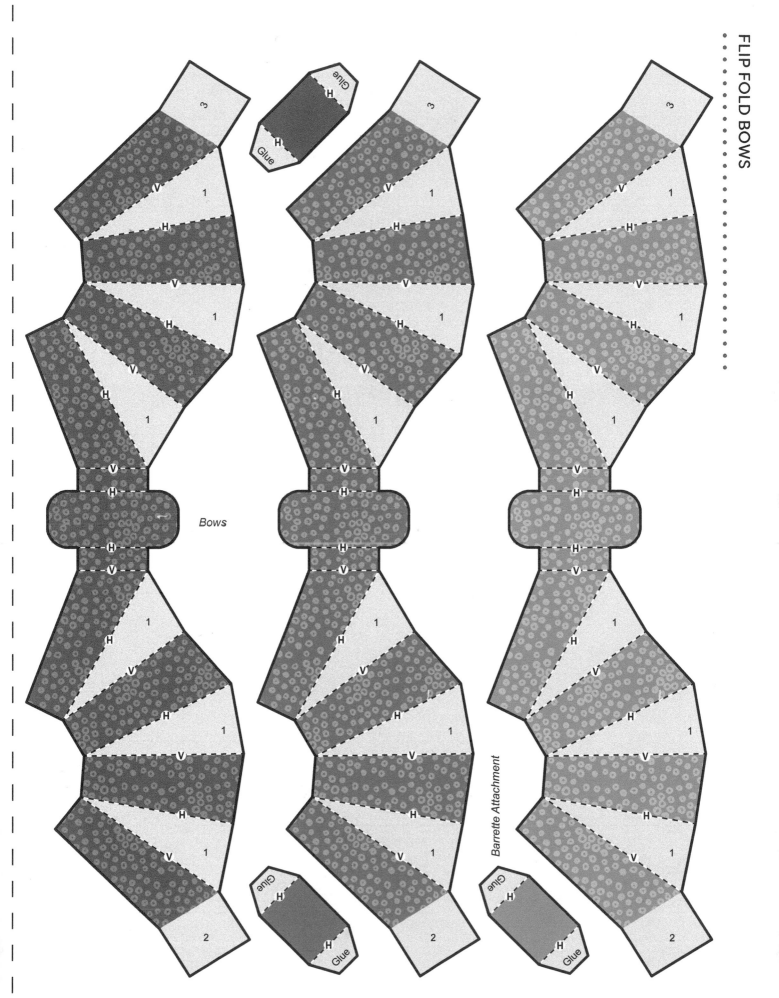

Bows

Barrette Attachment

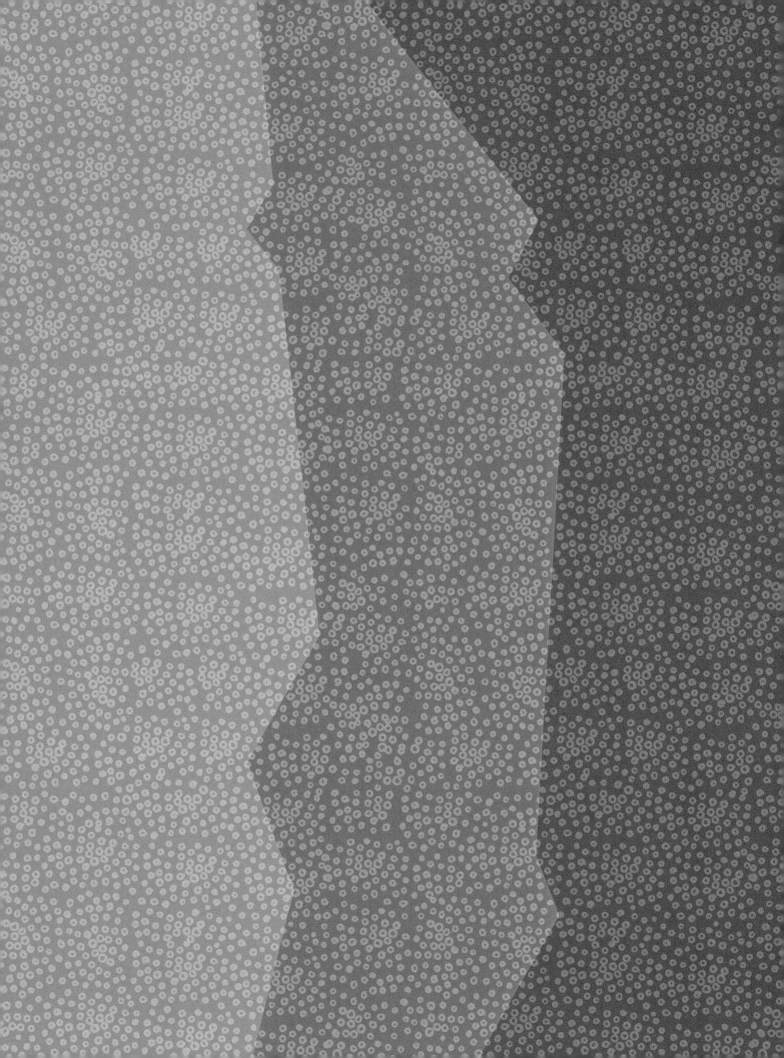

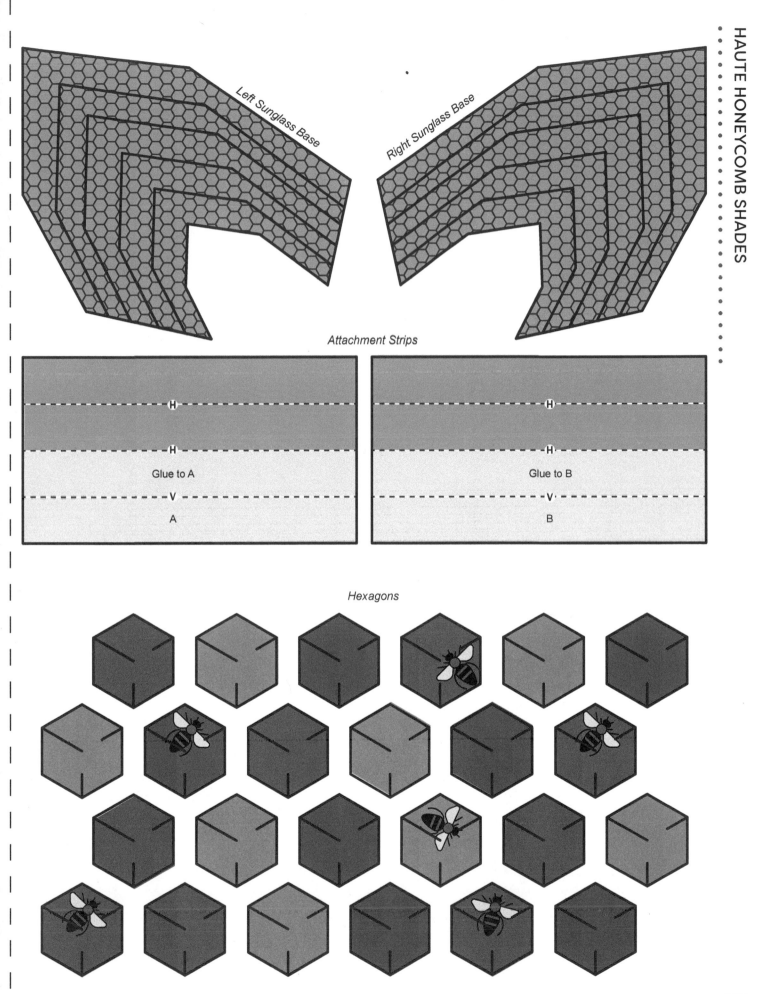

Left Sunglass Base

Right Sunglass Base

Attachment Strips

H

H

Glue to A

V

A

H

H

Glue to B

V

B

Hexagons

FRIENDLY FOX MASK

Attachment Strip

Section 4

Tape

Face

Glue to Left Ear

Glue to Left Ear

Glue to Right Ear

Glue to Right Ear

Right Ear

Left Ear

Nose

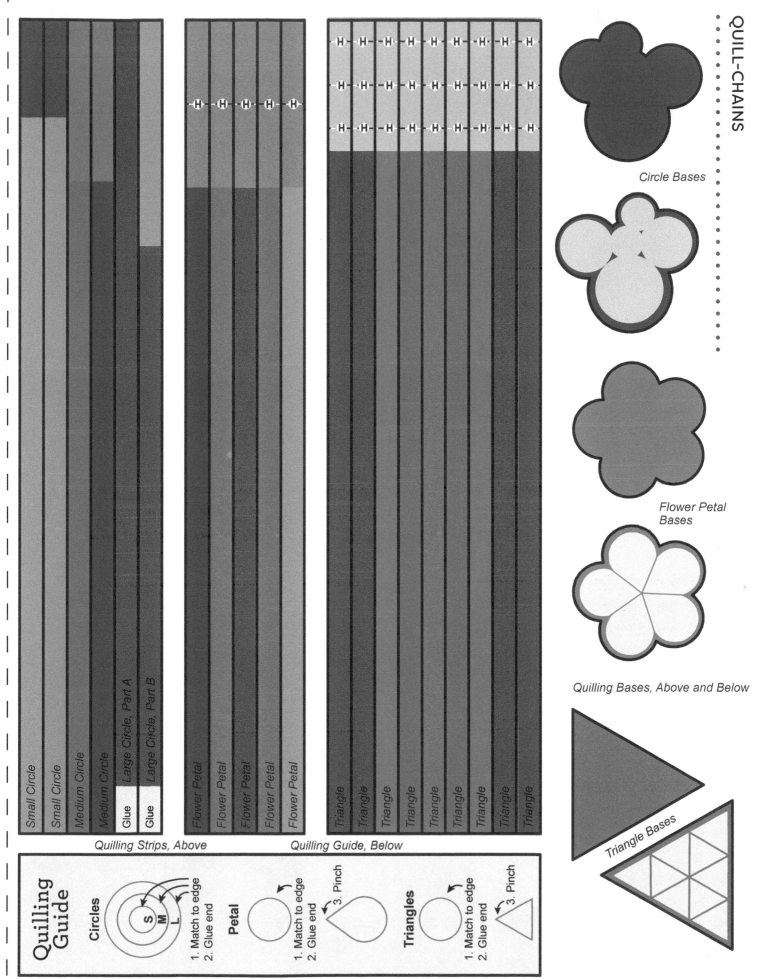

Circle Bases

Flower Petal Bases

Quilling Bases, Above and Below

Triangle Bases

Small Circle

Small Circle

Medium Circle

Medium Circle

Large Circle, Part A

Glue

Large Circle, Part B

Glue

Quilling Strips, Above

Flower Petal

Flower Petal

Flower Petal

Flower Petal

Flower Petal

Quilling Guide, Below

Triangle

Triangle

Triangle

Triangle

Triangle

Triangle

Triangle

Triangle

Triangle

Quilling Guide

Circles

S M L

1. Match to edge
2. Glue end

Petal

1. Match to edge
2. Glue end

3. Pinch

Triangles

1. Match to edge
2. Glue end

3. Pinch

59

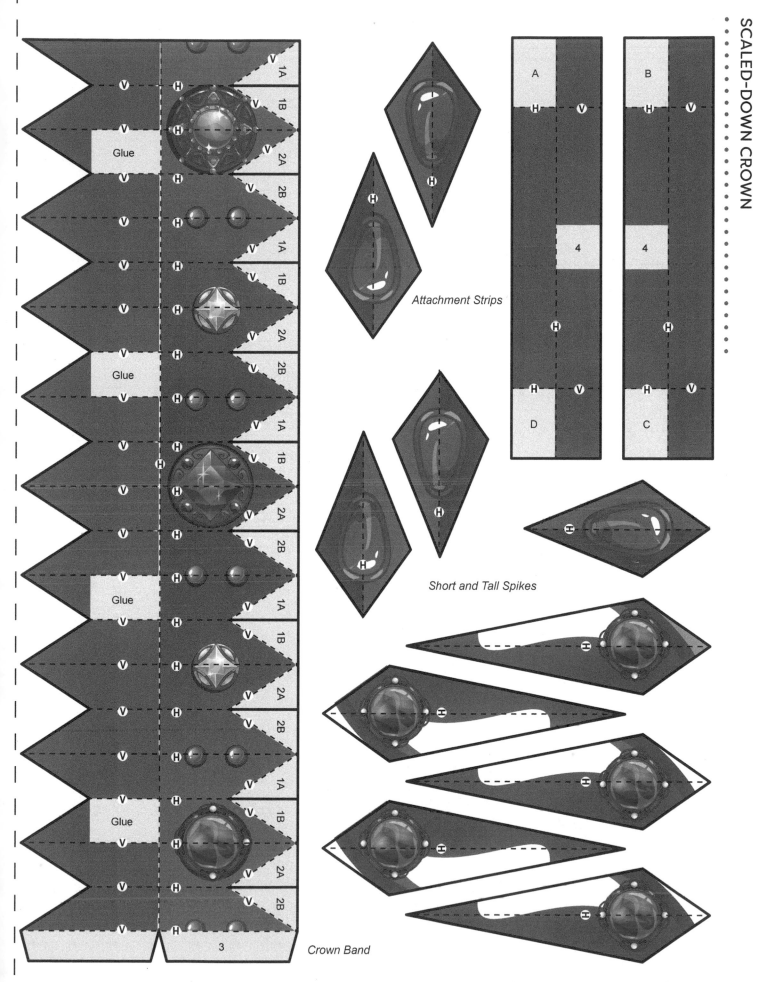

Attachment Strips

Short and Tall Spikes

Crown Band

Glue

A

B

4

4

D

C

1A
1B
2A
2B
1A
1B
2A
2B
1A
1B
2A
2B
1A
1B
2A
2B

3

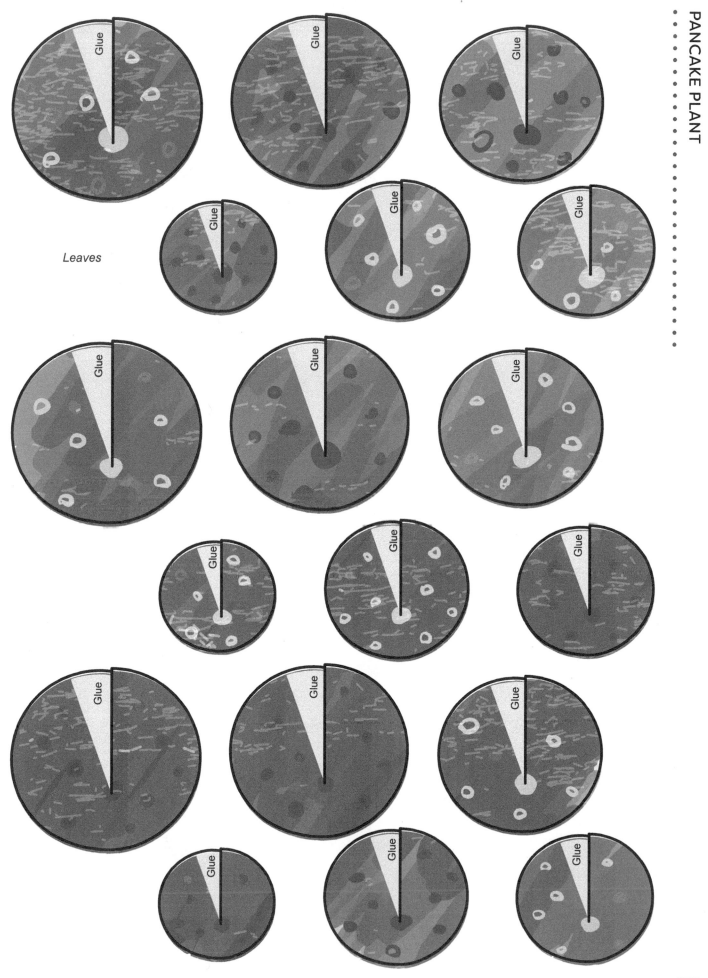

Leaves

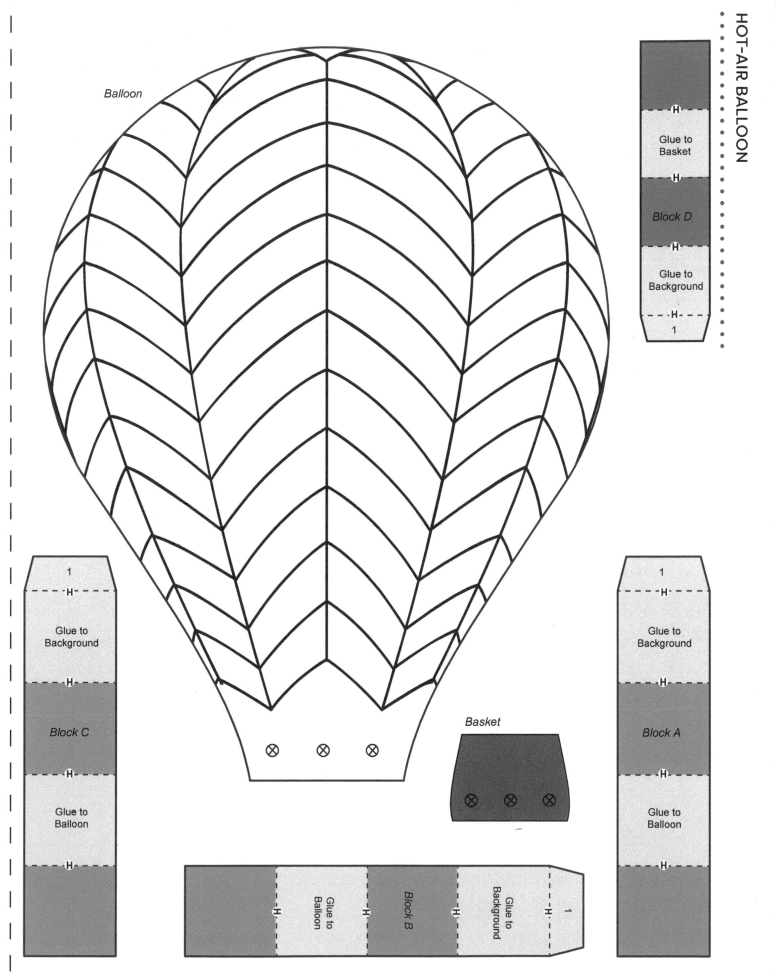

Balloon

Glue to Basket

Block D

Glue to Background

1

Glue to Background

Block C

Glue to Balloon

Glue to Background

Block A

Glue to Balloon

Basket

Glue to Balloon

Block B

Glue to Background

1

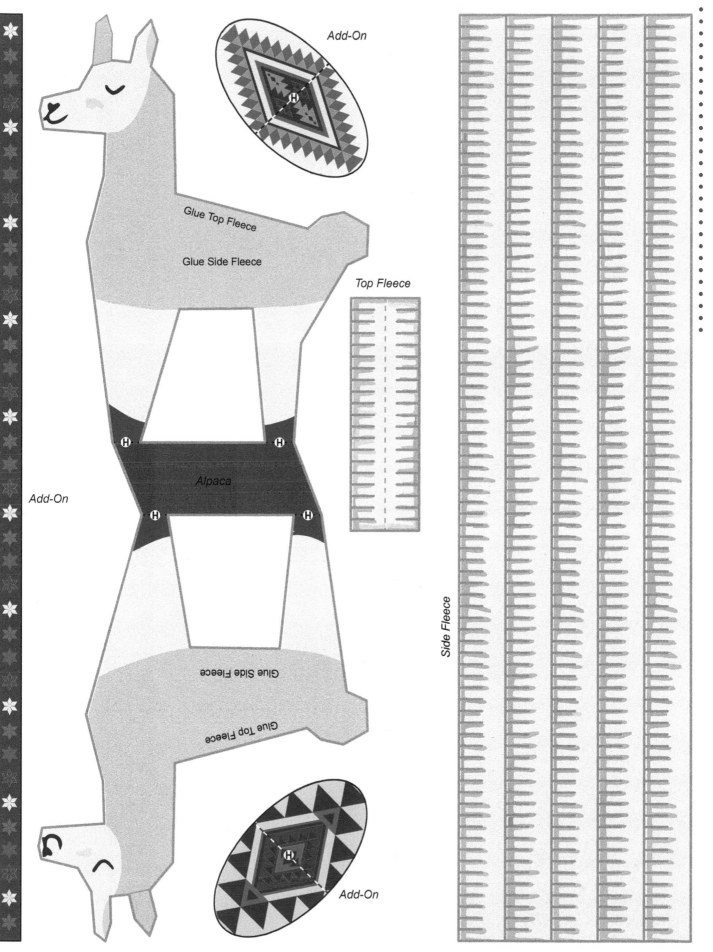

Add-On

Glue Top Fleece

Glue Side Fleece

Top Fleece

Alpaca

Add-On

Glue Side Fleece

Glue Top Fleece

Add-On

Side Fleece

Background, Above

Collage Pieces, Below

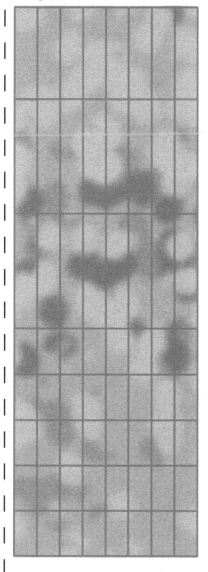
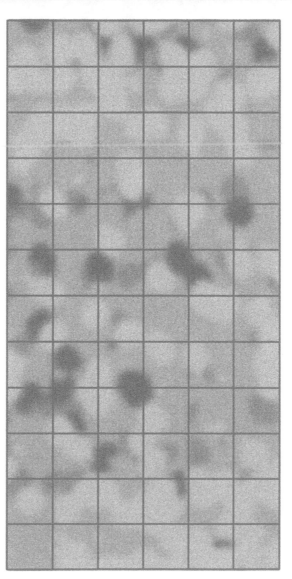
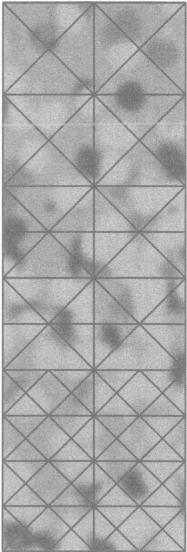

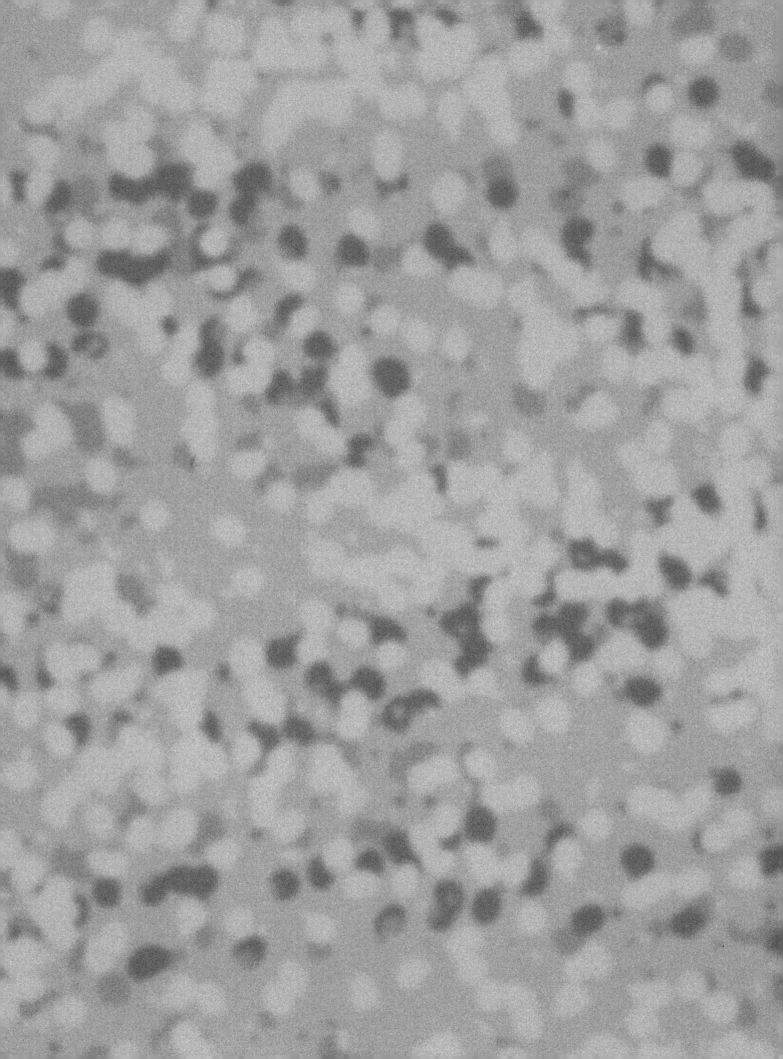

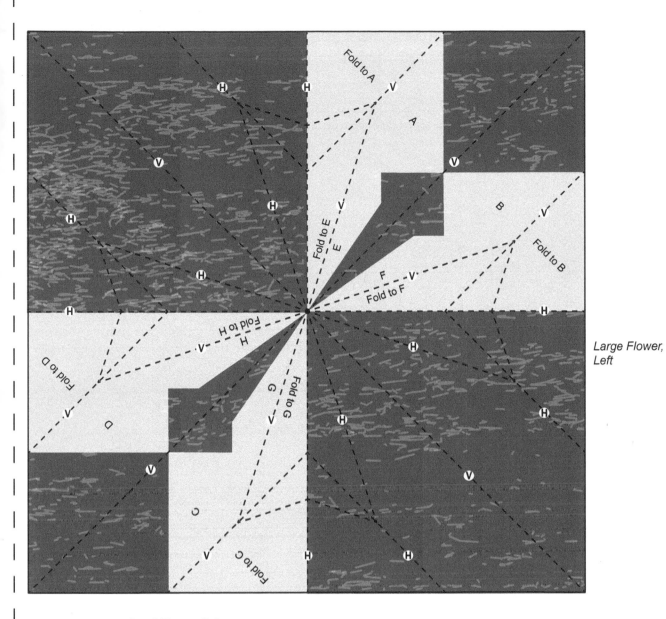

*Large Flower,
Left*

Small Flower, Below

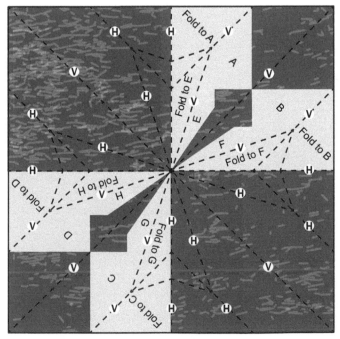

Small Flower, Below

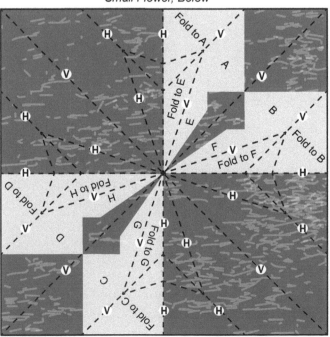

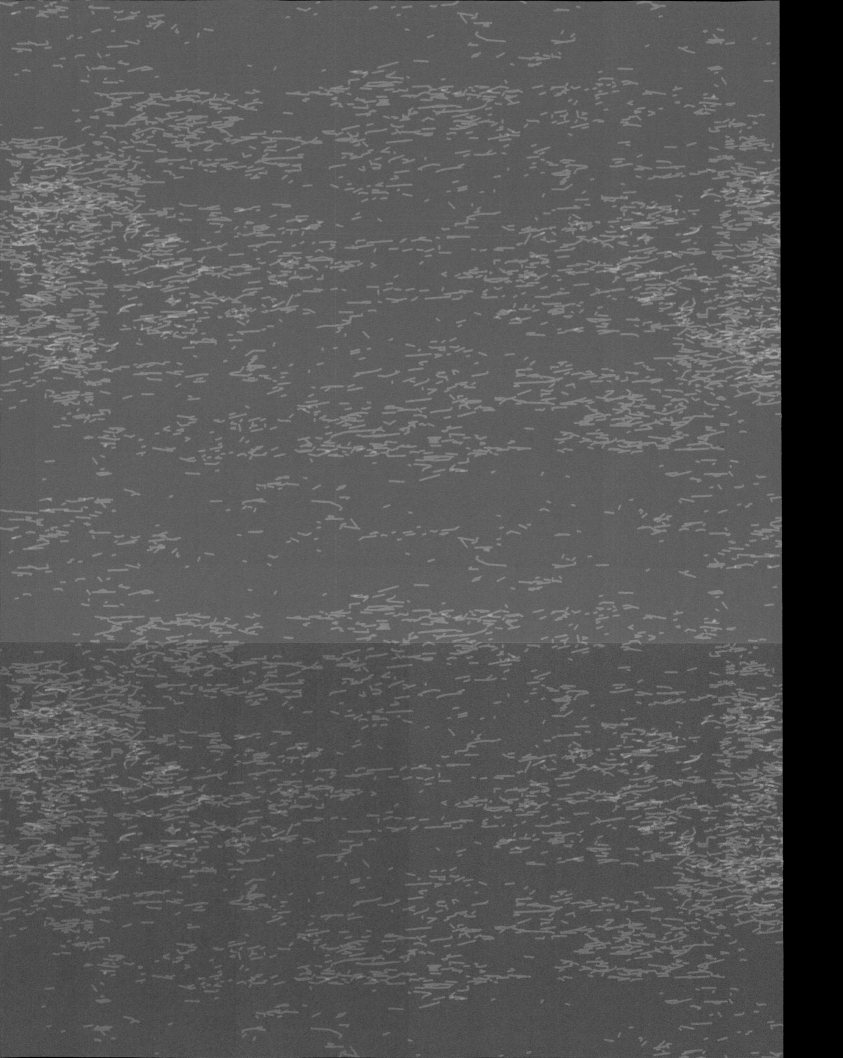

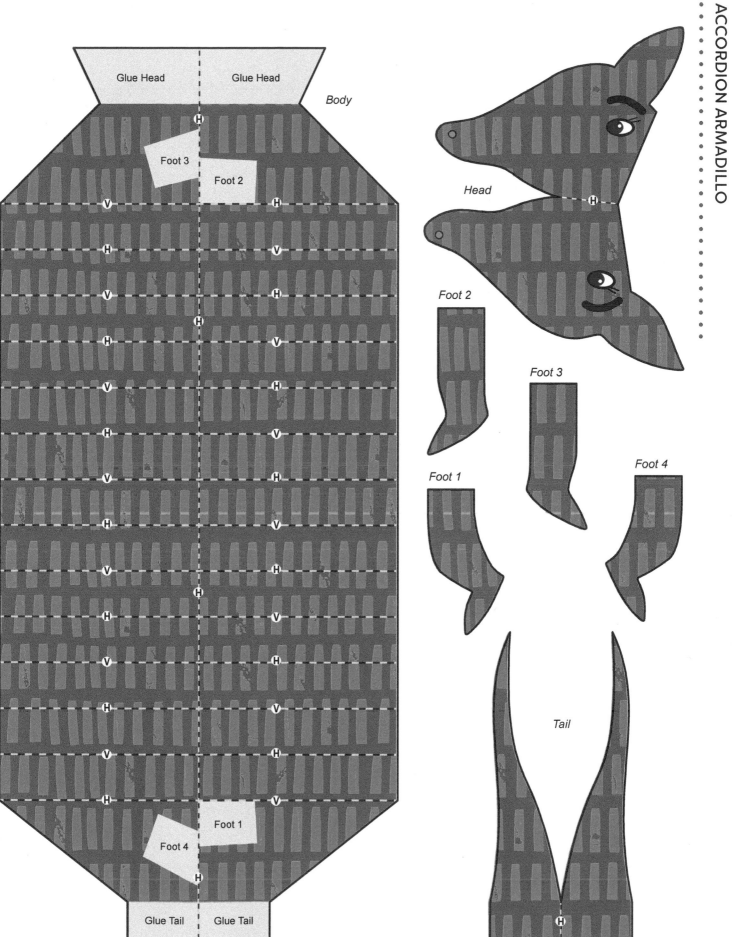

Glue Head

Glue Head

Body

Foot 3

Foot 2

Foot 1

Foot 4

Glue Tail

Glue Tail

Head

Foot 2

Foot 3

Foot 1

Foot 4

Tail

73

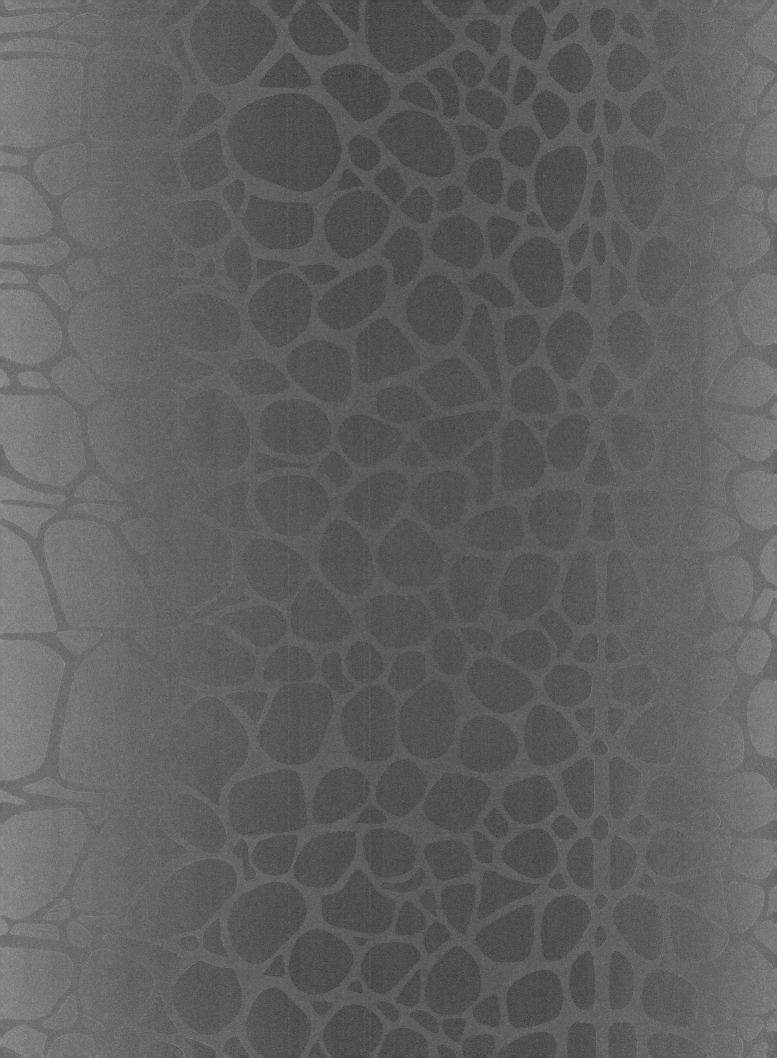

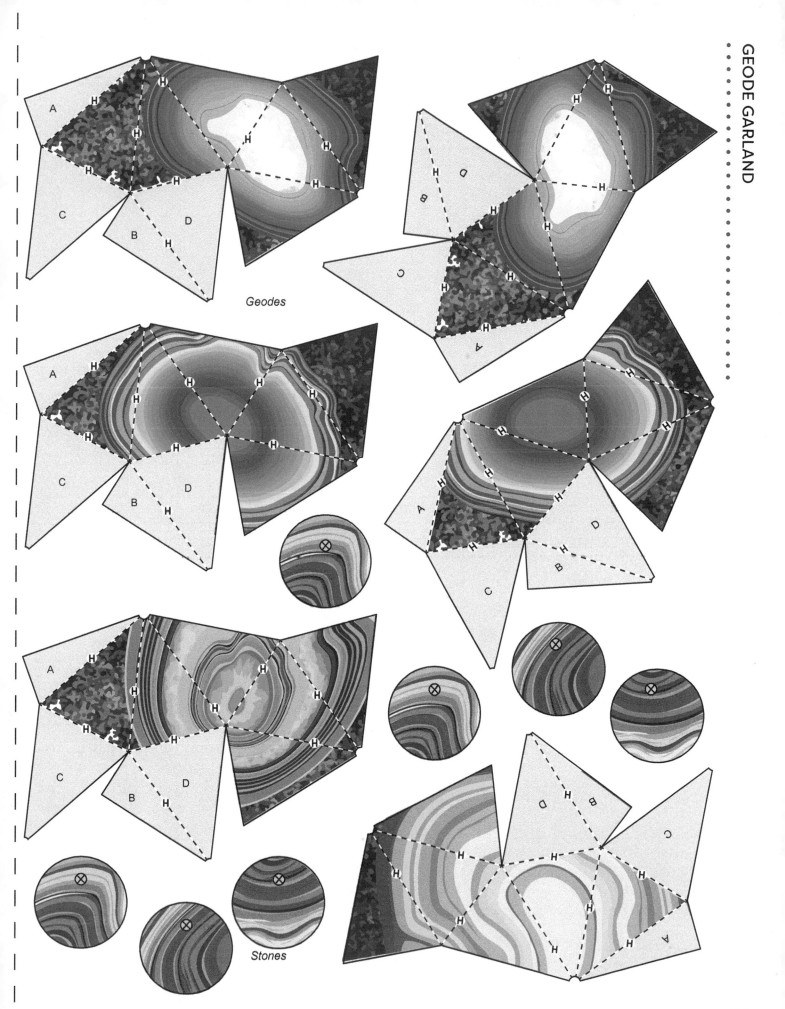

Geodes

Stones

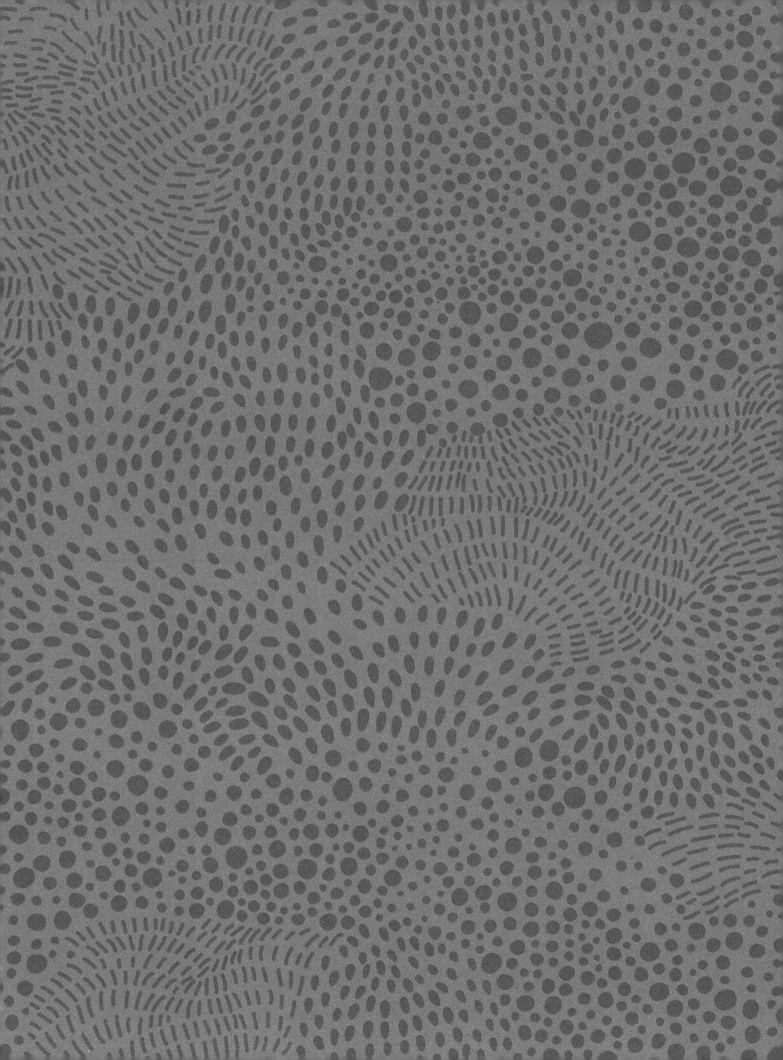

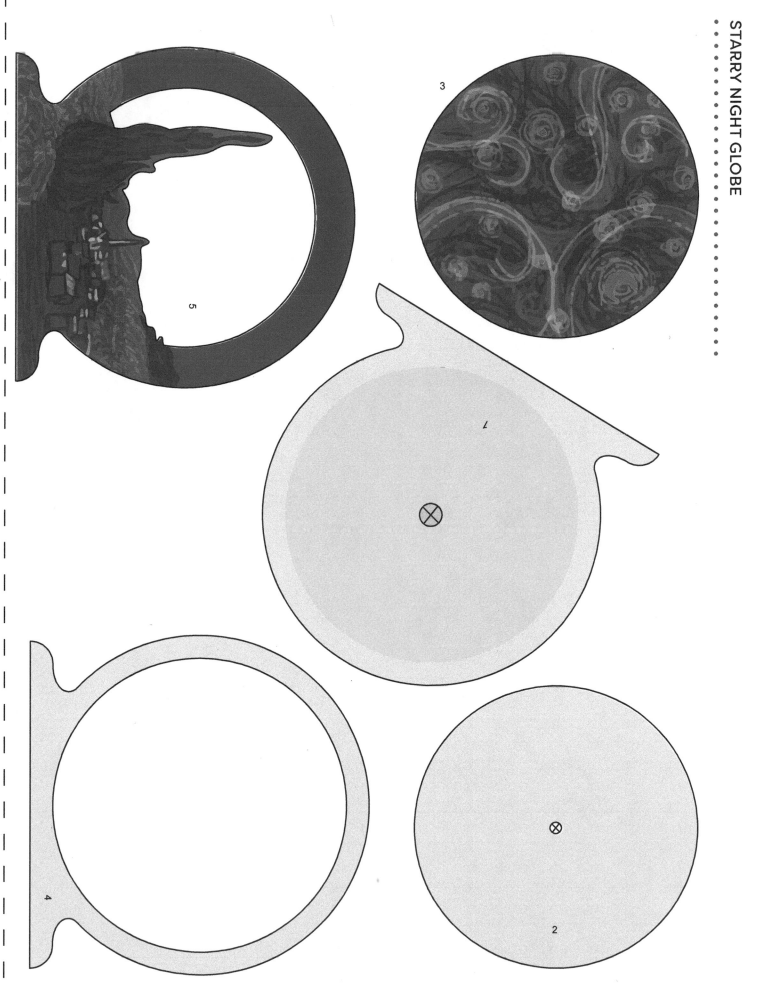

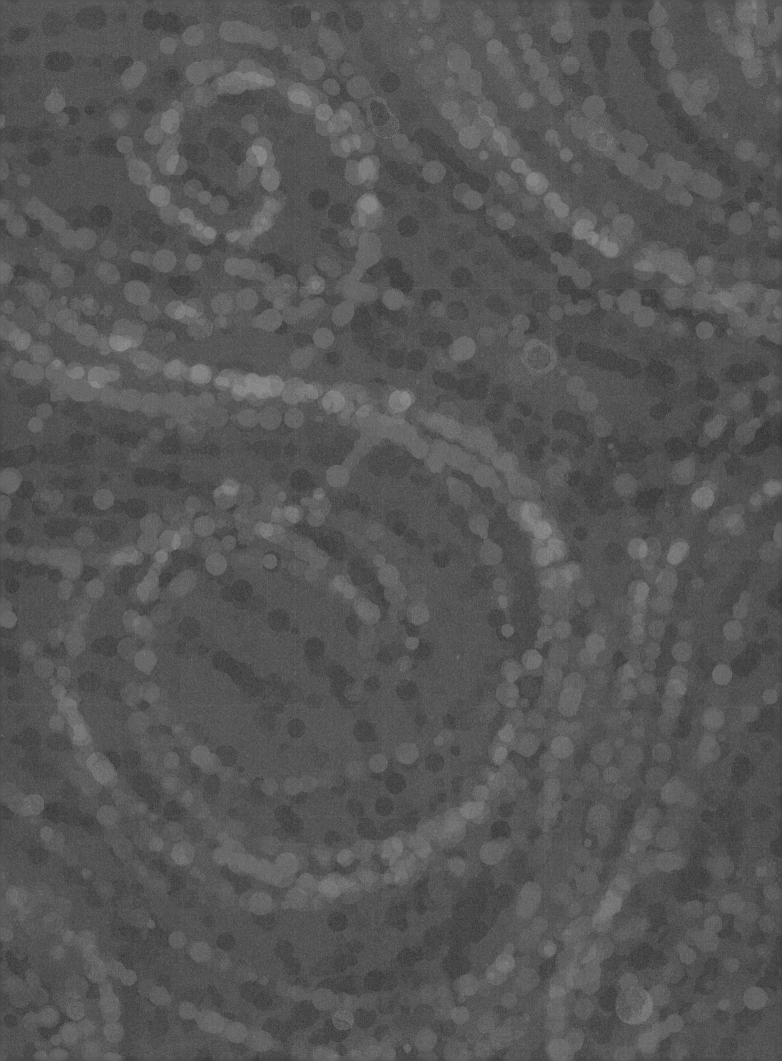

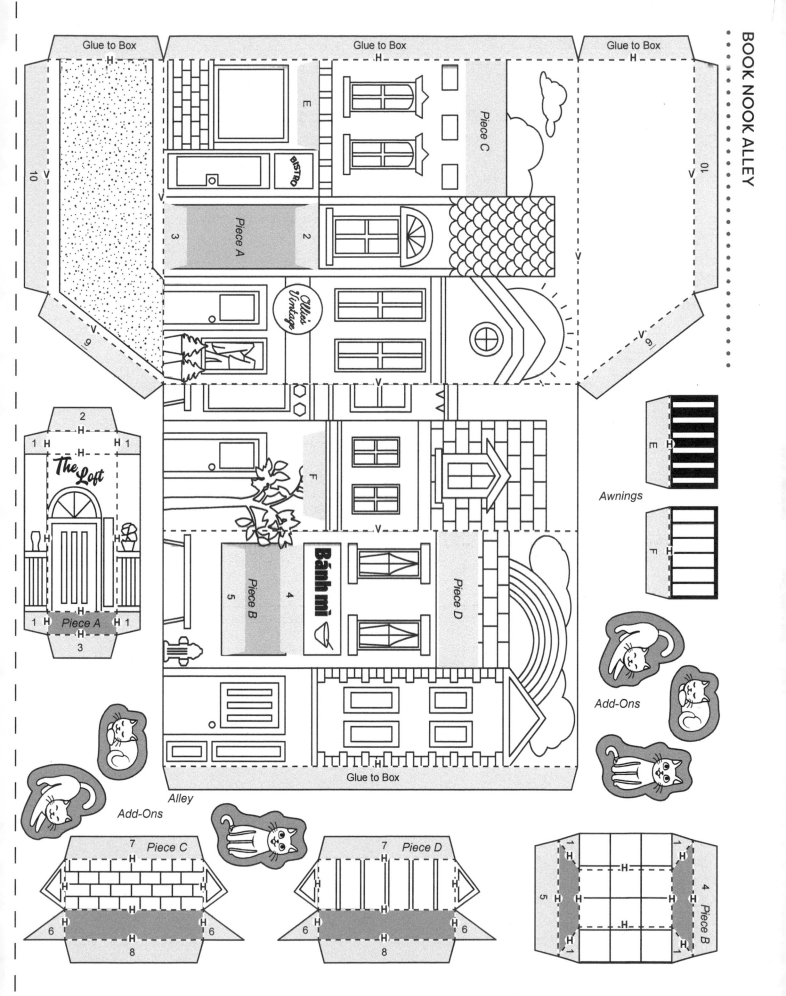

Base

Sail Skyscraper

Petra Pavilion

Triangle Tower

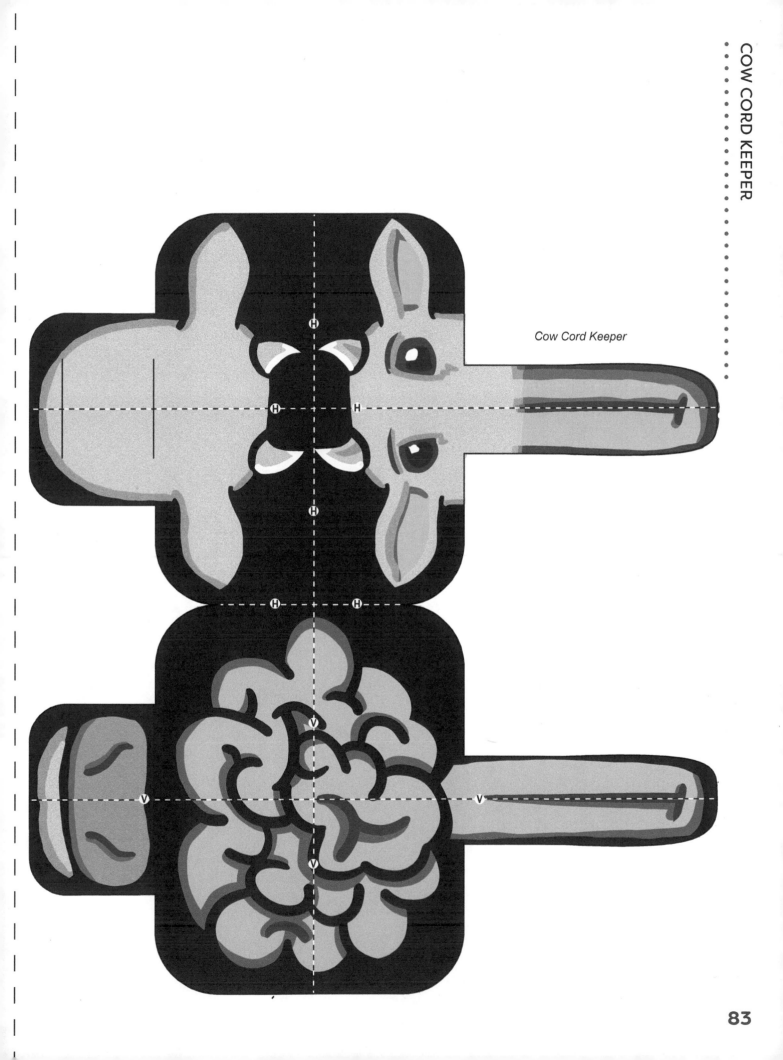

Cow Cord Keeper

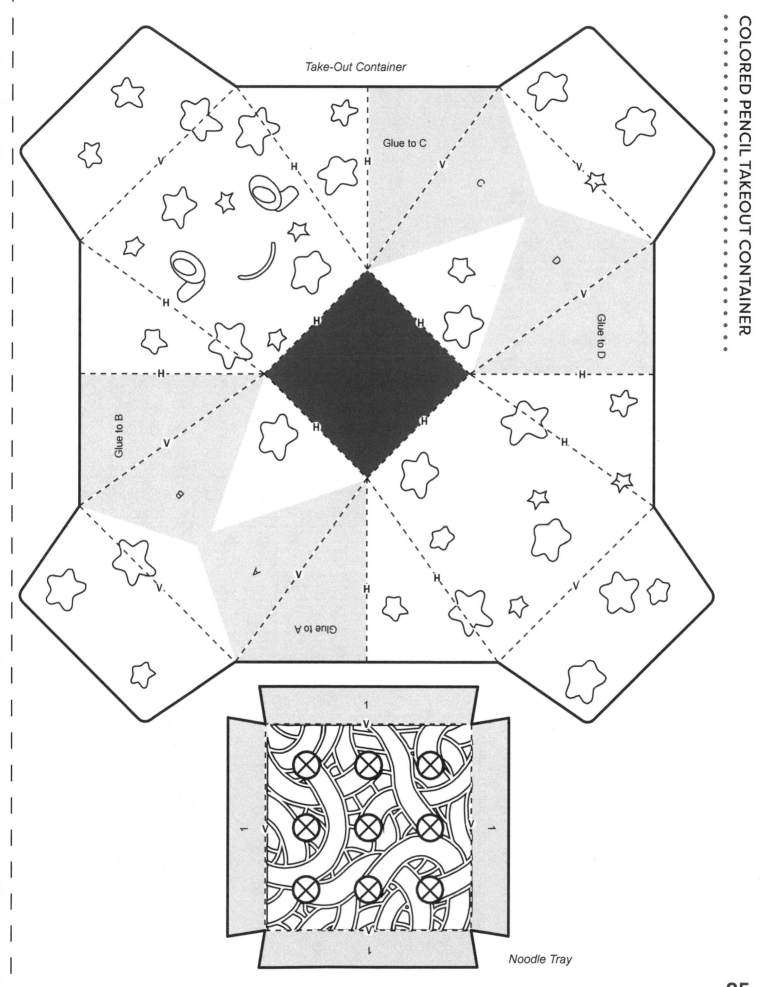

Take-Out Container

Glue to C

Glue to D

Glue to B

Glue to A

Noodle Tray

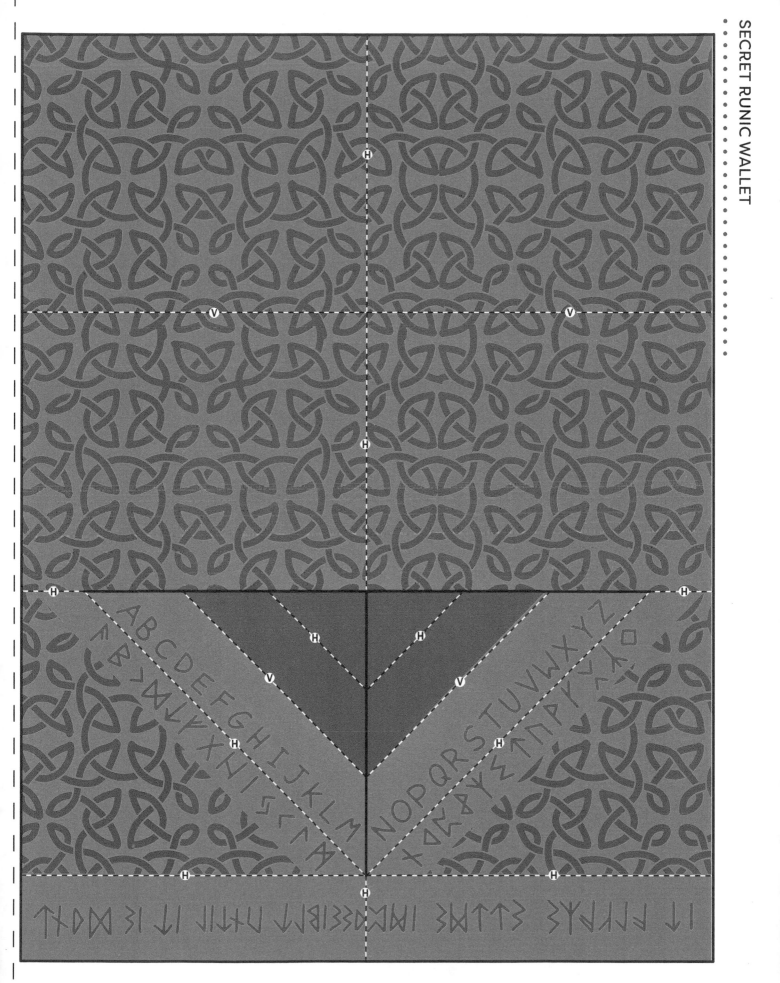

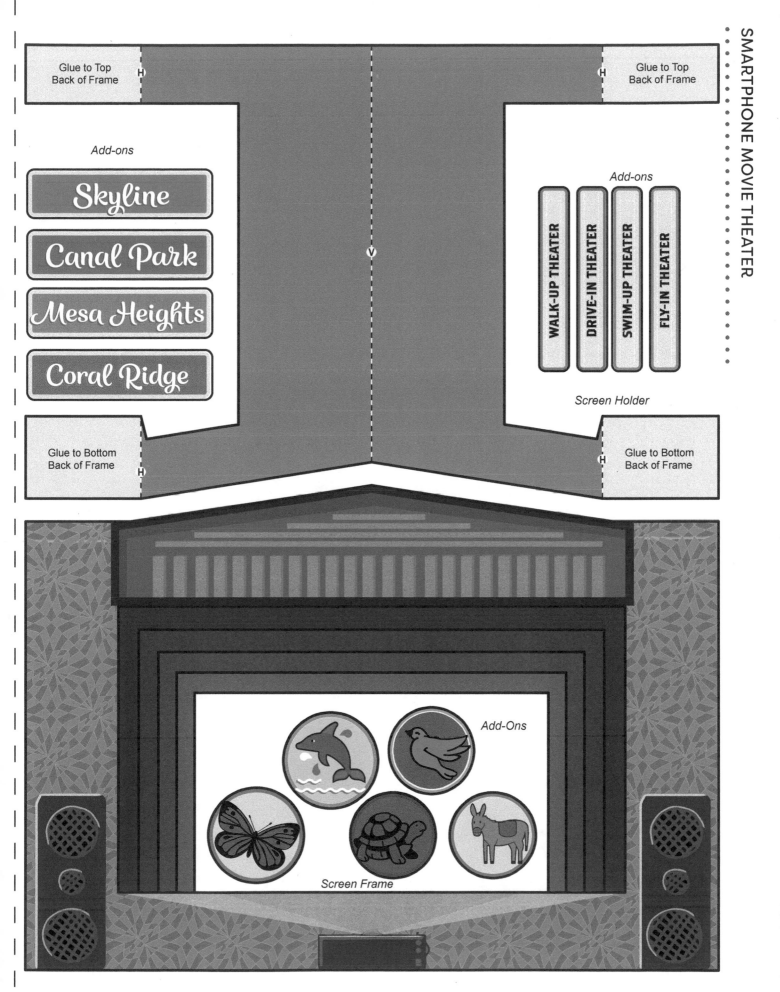

Glue to Top
Back of Frame

Glue to Top
Back of Frame

Add-ons

Skyline

Canal Park

Mesa Heights

Coral Ridge

Add-ons

WALK-UP THEATER

DRIVE-IN THEATER

SWIM-UP THEATER

FLY-IN THEATER

Screen Holder

Glue to Bottom
Back of Frame

Glue to Bottom
Back of Frame

Add-Ons

Screen Frame

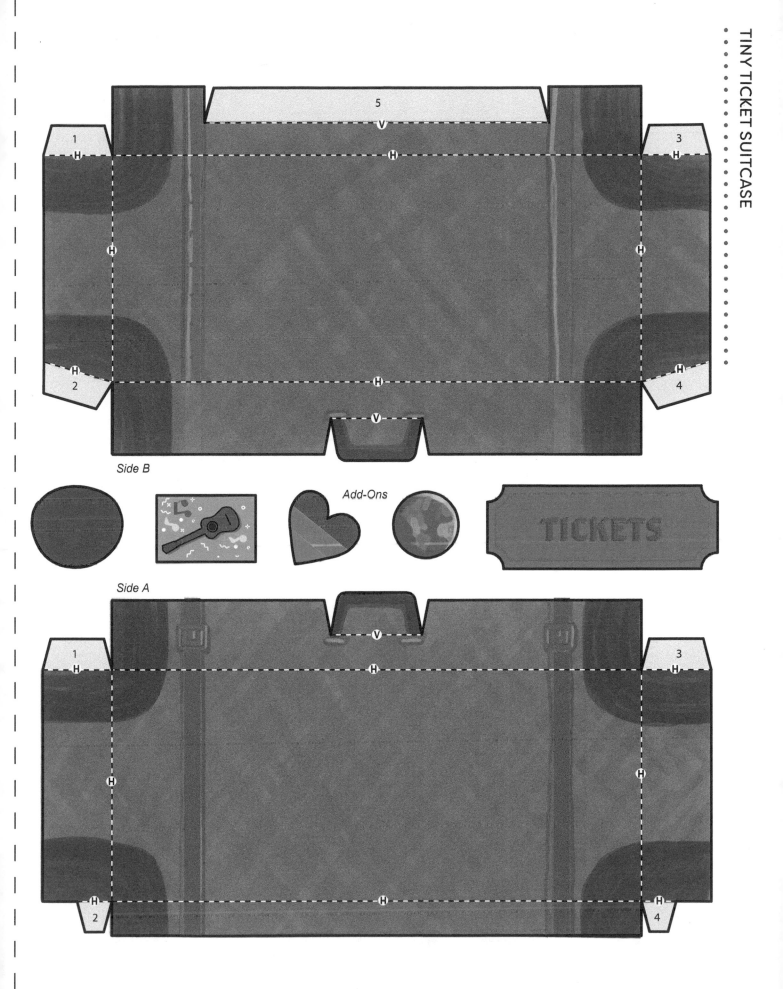

Side B

Add-Ons

TICKETS

Side A

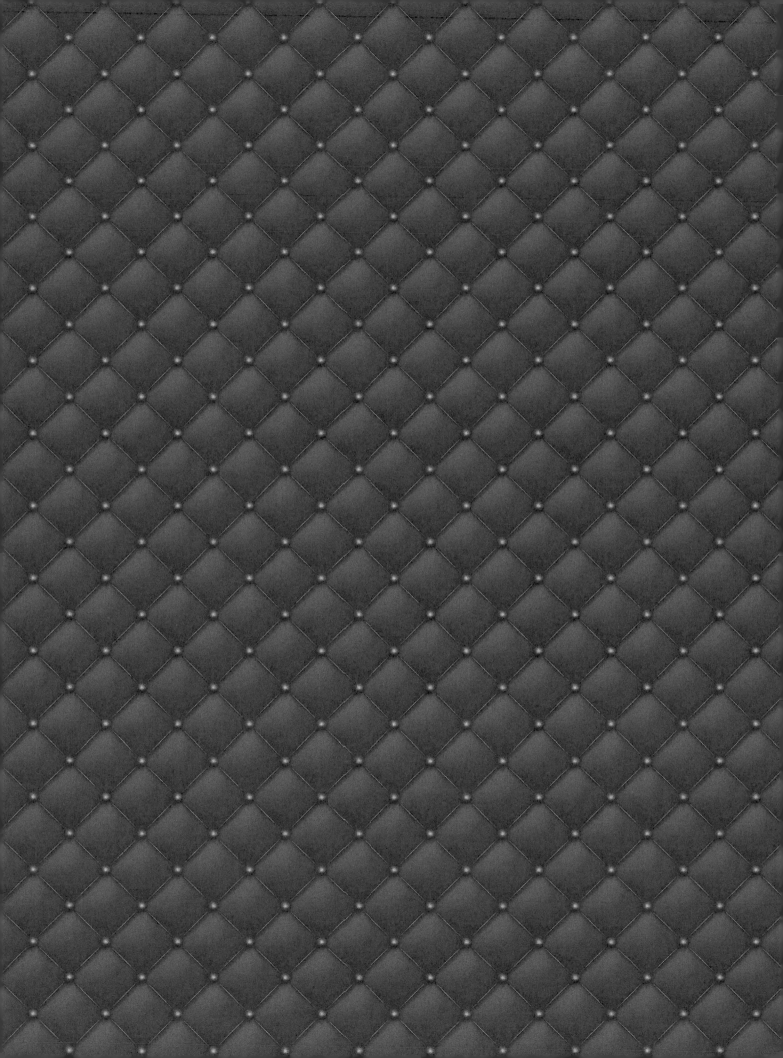

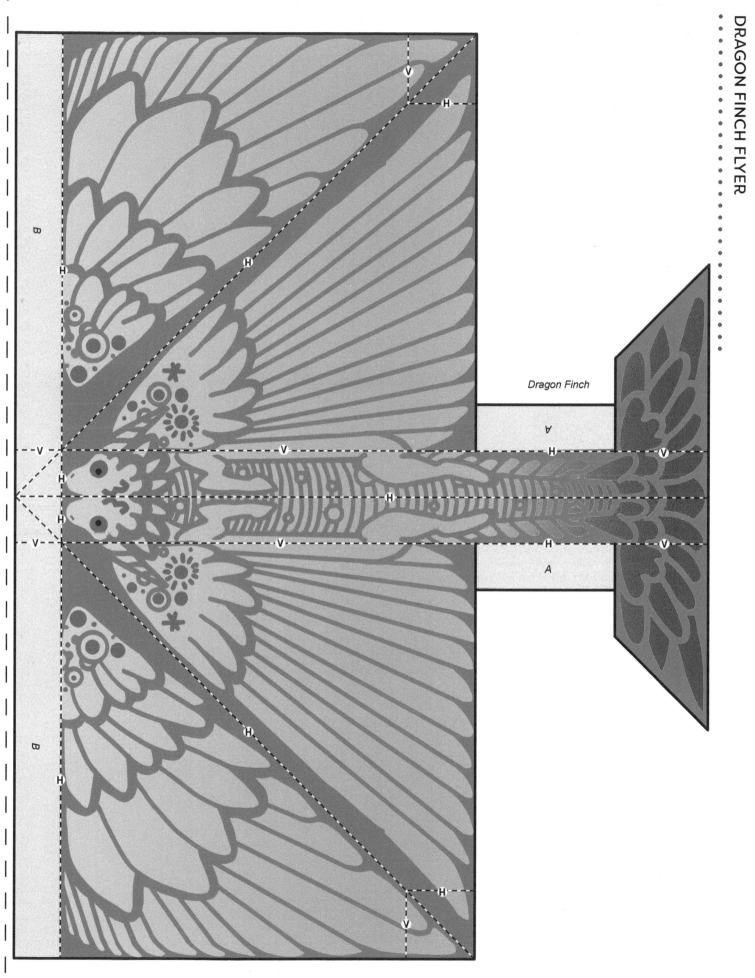

Dragon Finch

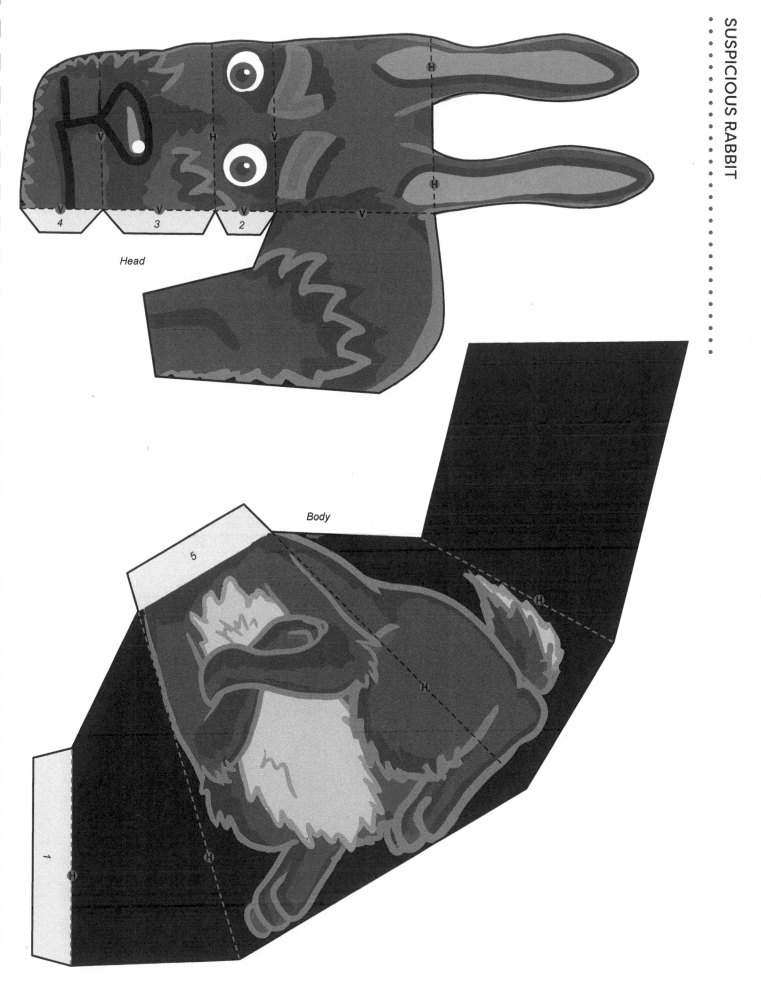

Head

Body

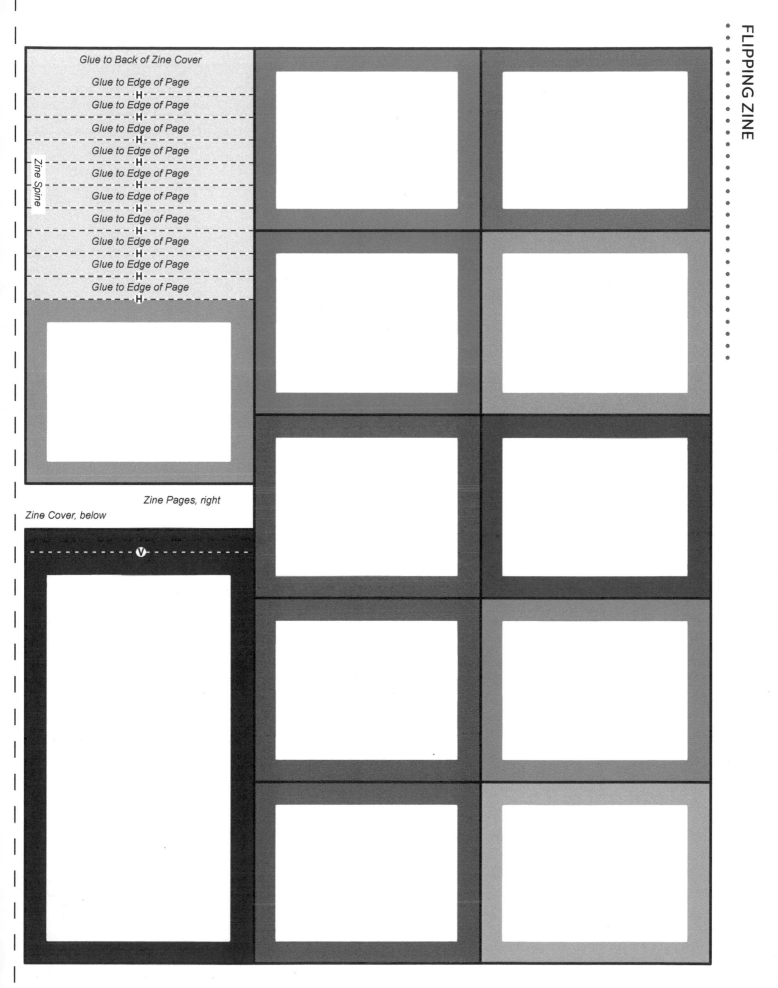

Glue to Back of Zine Cover

Glue to Edge of Page
·H·
Glue to Edge of Page
·H·
Glue to Edge of Page
·H·
Glue to Edge of Page
·H·
Glue to Edge of Page
·H·
Glue to Edge of Page

Glue to Edge of Page

Glue to Edge of Page
·H·
Glue to Edge of Page
·H·
Glue to Edge of Page
·H·

Zine Spine

Zine Pages, right

Zine Cover, below

·V·

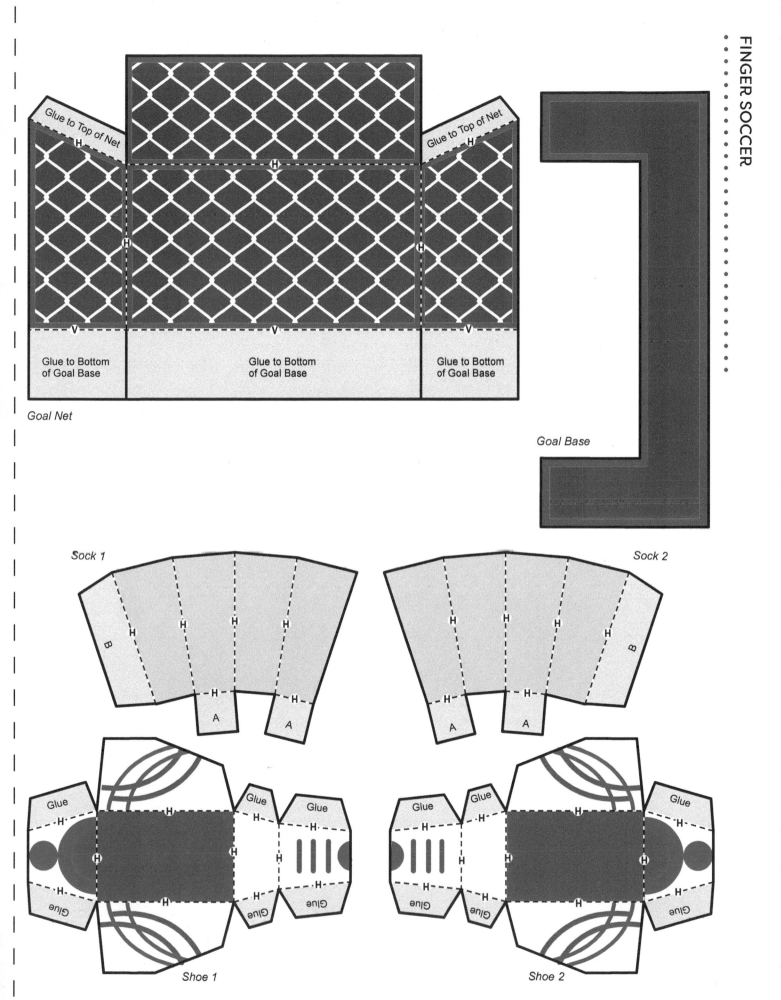

Goal Net

Glue to Top of Net

Glue to Top of Net

Glue to Bottom
of Goal Base

Glue to Bottom
of Goal Base

Glue to Bottom
of Goal Base

Goal Base

Sock 1

Sock 2

B

B

A

A

A

A

Glue

Glue

Glue

Glue

Glue

Glue

Glue

Glue

Shoe 1

Shoe 2

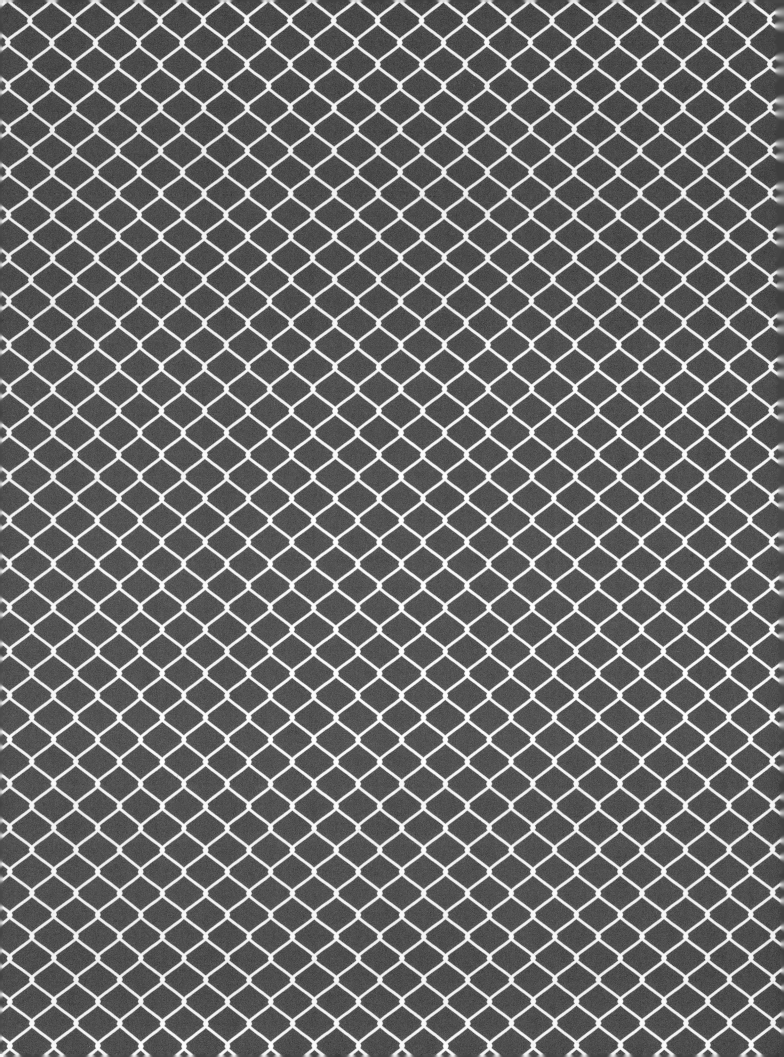

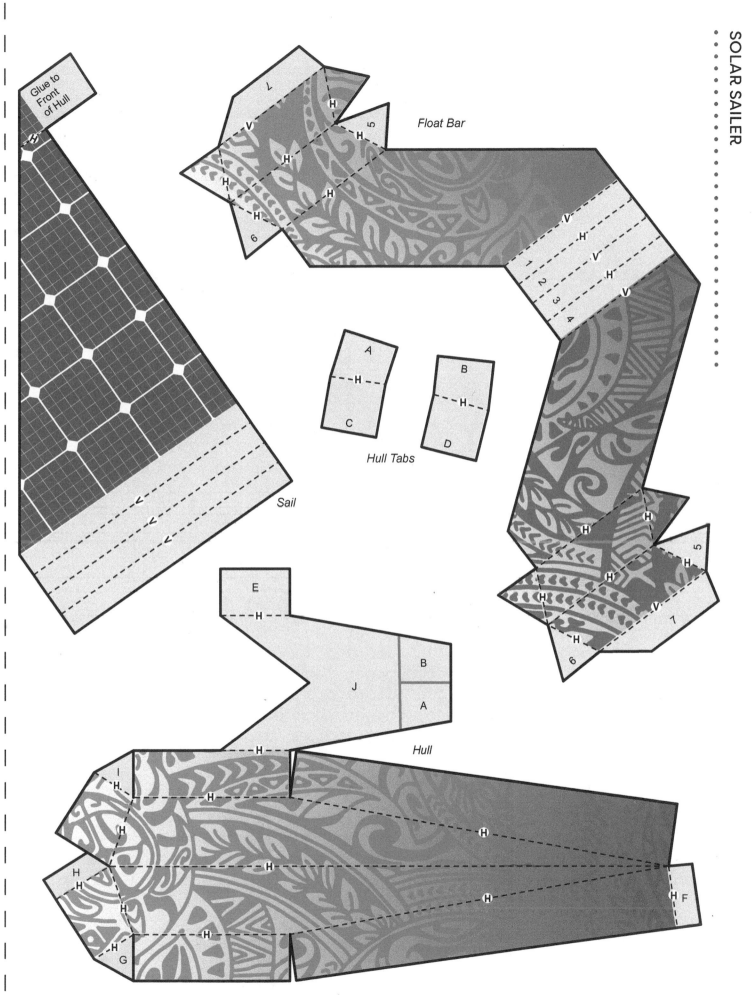

Glue to Front of Hull

Float Bar

Sail

Hull Tabs

Hull

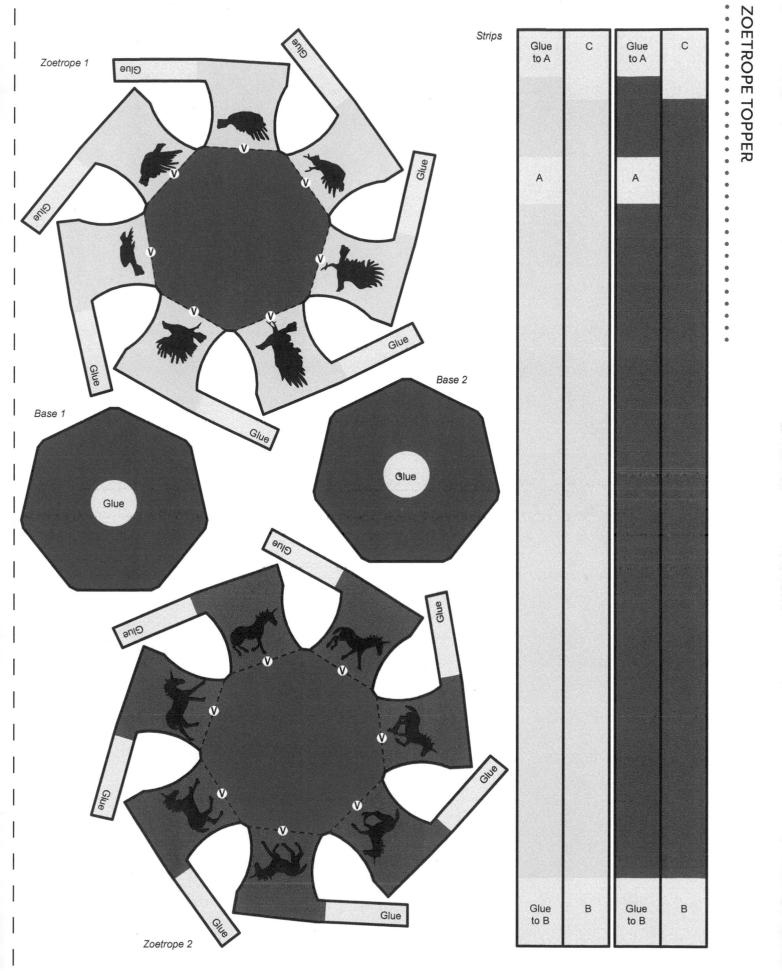

Zoetrope 1

Base 1

Glue

Base 2

Glue

Zoetrope 2

Strips

Glue to A	C	Glue to A	C
A		A	
Glue to B	B	Glue to B	B

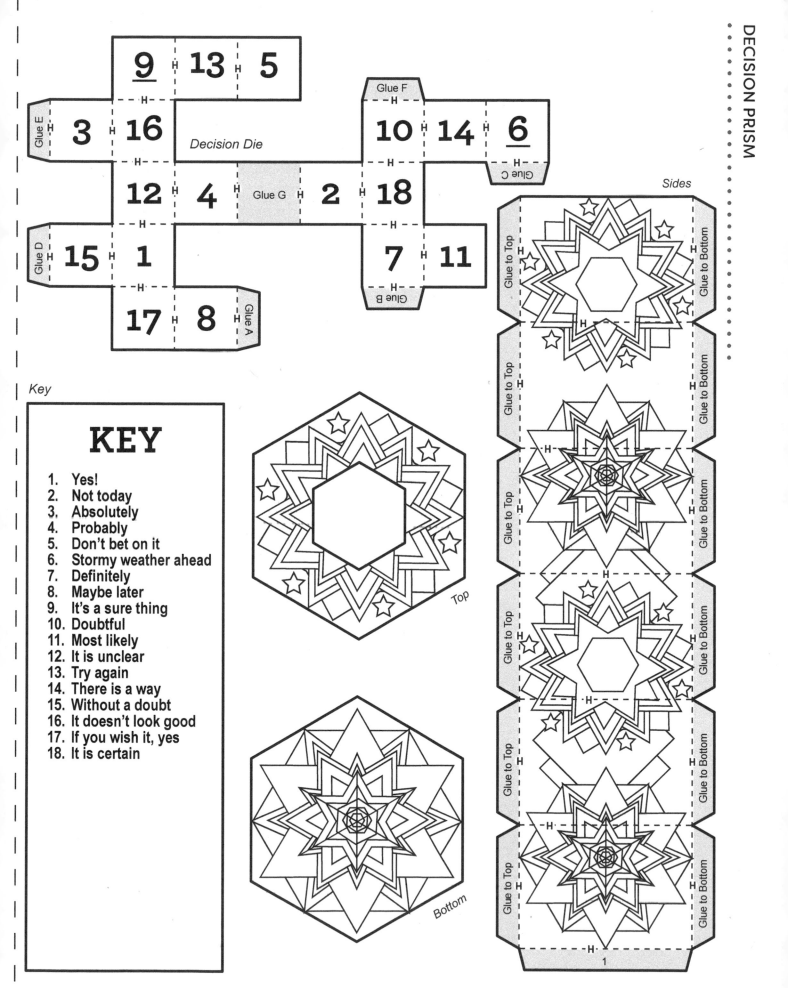

Decision Die

9	13	5
3	16	
12	4	2	18
15	1		7	11
17	8	
10	14	6

Glue E, Glue D, Glue A, Glue G, Glue B, Glue F, Glue C

Sides

Top

Bottom

KEY

1. Yes!
2. Not today
3. Absolutely
4. Probably
5. Don't bet on it
6. Stormy weather ahead
7. Definitely
8. Maybe later
9. It's a sure thing
10. Doubtful
11. Most likely
12. It is unclear
13. Try again
14. There is a way
15. Without a doubt
16. It doesn't look good
17. If you wish it, yes
18. It is certain

Glue to Top, Glue to Bottom

BONUS
TEMPLATES

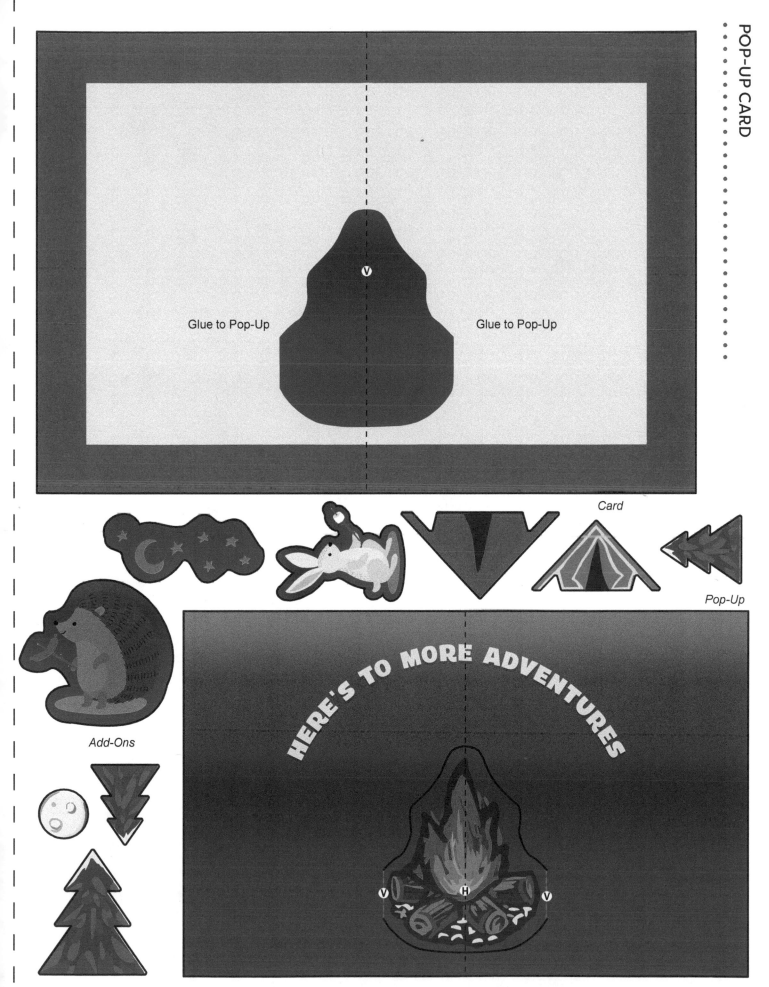

Glue to Pop-Up

Glue to Pop-Up

Card

Pop-Up

Add-Ons

HERE'S TO MORE ADVENTURES

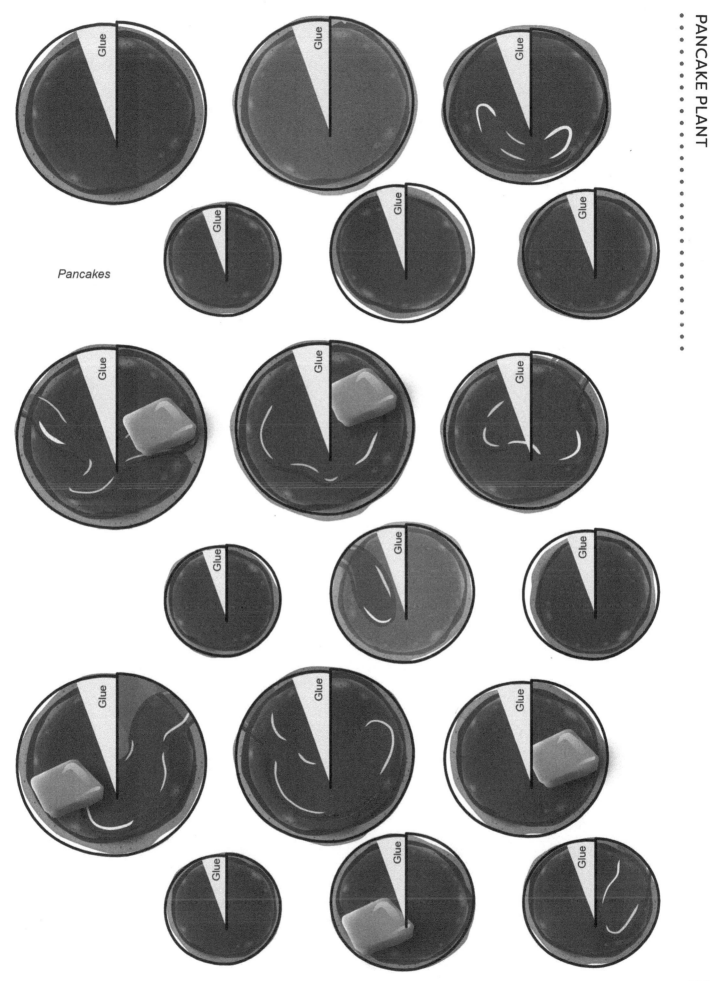

Pancakes

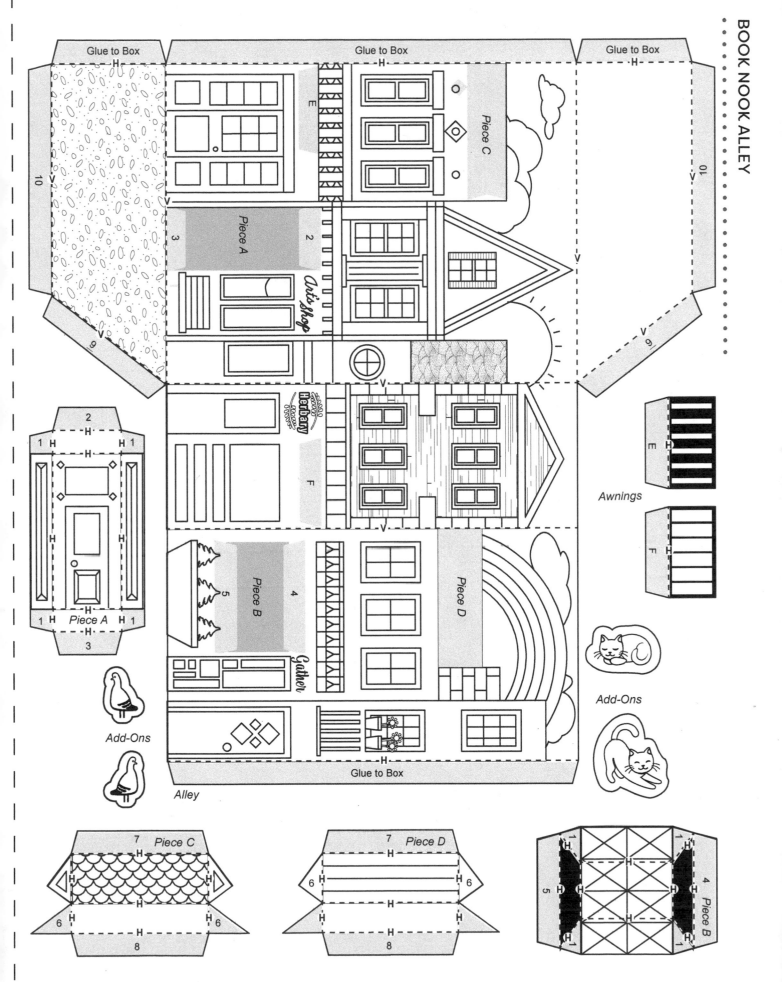

Glue to Box

Glue to Box

Glue to Box

Piece C

Piece A

Art's Shop

Herbary

Piece B

Piece D

Gather

Awnings

Piece A

Add-Ons

Add-Ons

Glue to Box

Alley

Piece C

Piece D

Piece B

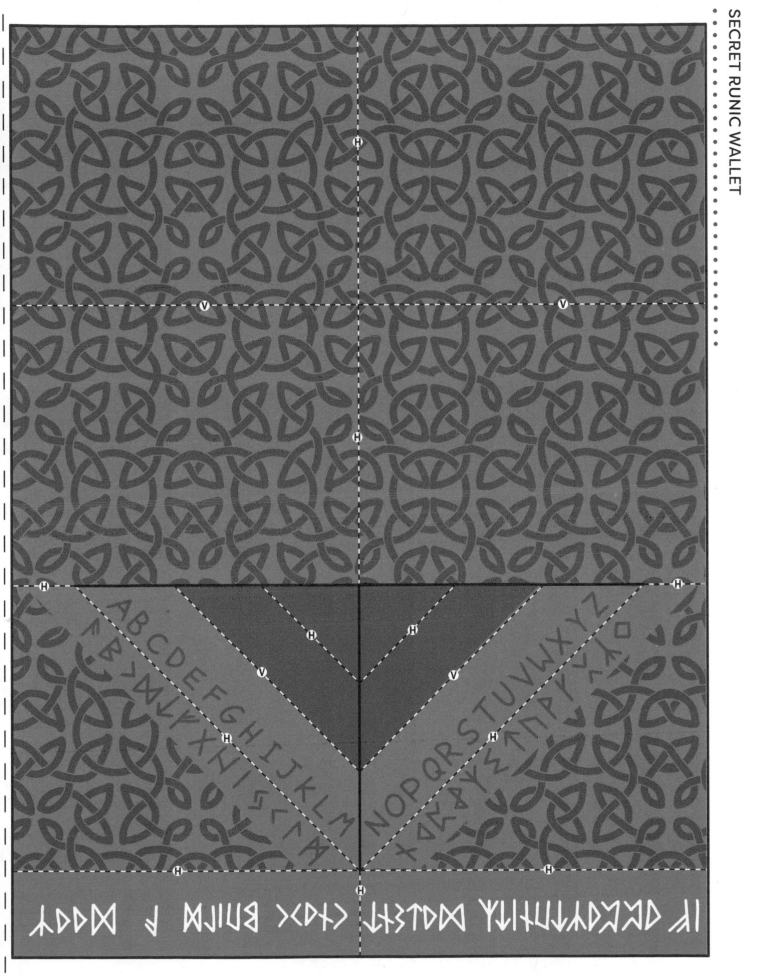

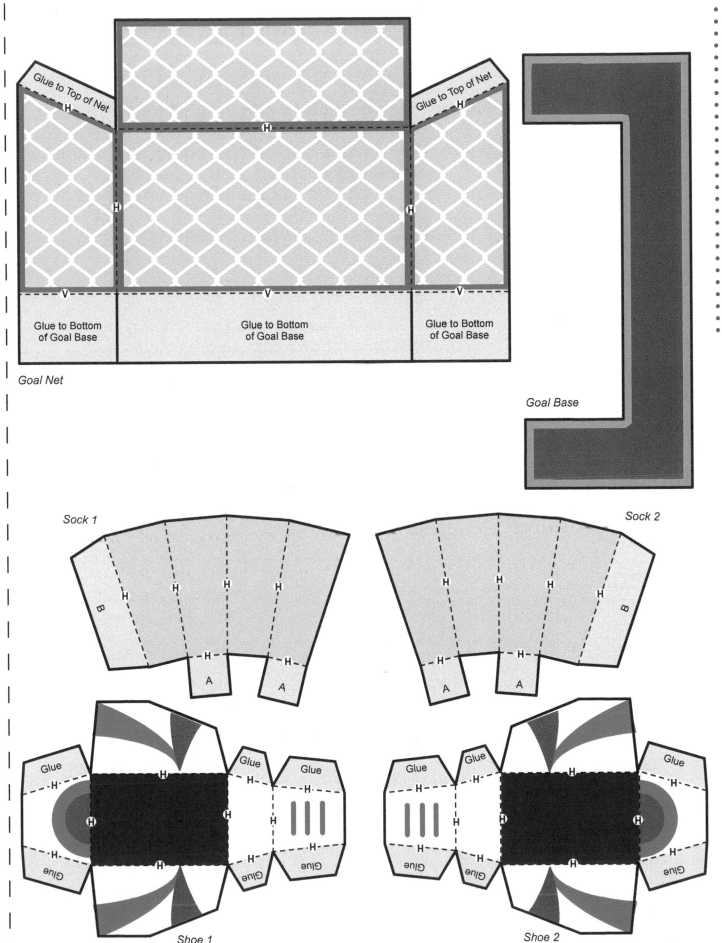

Glue to Top of Net

H

Glue to Top of Net

H

H

H

H

H

V

V

V

Glue to Bottom of Goal Base

Glue to Bottom of Goal Base

Glue to Bottom of Goal Base

Goal Net

Goal Base

Sock 1

Sock 2

B

H

H

H

H

H

A

H

H

A

H

H

H

H

B

A

H

A

Glue

H

H

Glue

Glue

H

H

H

Glue

Glue

Glue

H

Glue

H

H

Glue

H

Glue

H

H

H

H

H

H

H

Glue

H

H

Glue

Shoe 1

Shoe 2

ACKNOWLEDGMENTS

Thank you:

Denise and Martin Glover, and my family, who nurtured my creativity.

Derek Williams, who remains ever positive no matter how many folded papers fill our apartment.

Paul Jackson, Kunihiko Kasahara, Jerry Andrus, and countless other paper crafters whose willingness to share ideas sparked the flame of form for these projects.

Mary Colgan, Joe Cho, Laura Apperson, and everyone else on my publishing team who brought this kismet dream to life.

And my students, who remind me every day that the object of life is play.

ABOUT THE AUTHOR

LISA GLOVER holds degrees in architecture and engineering from Lehigh University. She is a multifaceted artist and the Maker in Residence at the Stourbridge Project in Honesdale, Pennsylvania. She lives with her partner, Derek, and their two twin rabbits. For more fun projects and inspiring creations, visit LisatheMaker.com.